# STREETWISE

## UPPER-INTERMEDIATE
### Student's Book

**Rob Nolasco**

Oxford University Press

# LANGUAGE INPUT

| | Part | Page | Topic | Grammar | Function | Vocabulary |
|---|---|---|---|---|---|---|
| **ISSUE 1** | 1 | 2 | Shop talk | Present tenses<br>Adverbs of frequency | | Words in context<br>Shops and shopping |
| | 2 | 4 | Food glorious food | *feel/look/seem/smell/sound/taste*<br>Questions with *like* | Compliments | Words in context<br>Describing food |
| | 3 | 6 | Yours | Agreement of verbs and subjects | | |
| | Over to you! | 8 | Consumer surveys | | | |
| **ISSUE 2** | 1 | 10 | Class mates! | Present perfect simple and progressive<br>*school* or *the school* | | Words in context<br>Jobs and qualifications |
| | 2 | 12 | Last chance | Definite, indefinite, and zero article | Making/responding to suggestions | Words in context |
| | 3 | 14 | Dear Sir/Madam | | | |
| | Language awareness | 16 | Our view of the world | | | Expressions with *time* |

17–20 Grammar review Issues 1 and 2; Grammar practice; Wise up! – Vocabulary

| | Part | Page | Topic | Grammar | Function | Vocabulary |
|---|---|---|---|---|---|---|
| **ISSUE 3** | 1 | 22 | Rescue | Past tenses | | Words in context<br>Disasters |
| | 2 | 24 | Britain's naughtiest child? | Future in the past | Expressing opinions | Words in context; phrasal verbs; *dis-* and *mis-* |
| | 3 | 26 | Between the lines | Adjective + preposition combinations | | Adverbs |
| | Over to you! | 28 | Here is the news | | | |
| **ISSUE 4** | 1 | 30 | Faith in the future? | Future forms; *I hope so* and *I hope not* | | Words in context |
| | 2 | 32 | The big day | Future forms (present tenses used to express the future) | Expressing fear and anxiety | Phrasal verbs |
| | 3 | 34 | The inevitable gap? | | | Telephone expressions |
| | Language awareness | 36 | Rhythm and stress | | | |

37–40 Grammar review Issues 3 and 4; Grammar practice; Wise up! – Grammar

| | Part | Page | Topic | Grammar | Function | Vocabulary |
|---|---|---|---|---|---|---|
| **ISSUE 5** | 1 | 42 | Visitors from space | Passives | | Words in context<br>Prefixes *extra/astro/inter* |
| | 2 | 44 | Right to be left | Passive structures for modals<br>Prepositions with *agree* | Expressing reservations | Directional words |
| | 3 | 46 | What is your reaction time? | | | Instructional words |
| | Over to you! | 48 | A question of culture | | | |
| **ISSUE 6** | 1 | 50 | Leaders | Conditionals with *if* and *unless* | | Words in context<br>Leaders |
| | 2 | 52 | I wish I were … | *wish + would*<br>*wish + simple past* | Expressing surprise and disbelief | Words in context<br>Phrasal verbs |
| | 3 | 54 | Words of wisdom | | | *advice/advise*; *bored/boring*; *shy/shyness*, etc. |
| | Language awareness | 56 | Politeness | | | |

57–60 Grammar review Issues 5 and 6; Grammar practice; Wise up! – Reading

# SKILLS DEVELOPMENT

| Reading | Listening | Writing | Speaking | Pronunciation | |
|---|---|---|---|---|---|
| Intensive reading | Listening for information | Preparing a questionnaire | Class survey | | ISSUE 1 |
| | Inference and identifying expressions used | | | Intonation | ISSUE 1 |
| Reading for gist | | Writing a personal letter | Discussion – living in a foreign country | | ISSUE 1 |
| Reading for gist | | Research task – a consumer test | Discussion – designing a consumer test | | ISSUE 1 |
| | Listening for infomation | Guided text writing | Discussion – attitudes to different generations | Sentence stress | ISSUE 2 |
| Intensive reading | Listening for main points and expressions used | | Discussion – endangered species | *the* –/ði:/ or /ðə/ | ISSUE 2 |
| Reading for style and to spot errors | | Writing a formal letter of application | Discussion – personal qualities; role-play | | ISSUE 2 |
| Reading for information | | Research task – proverbs | | | ISSUE 2 |
| Intensive reading | | Writing a story | | Word-linking and intonation | ISSUE 3 |
| Intensive reading | Listening for information and expressions used | | Discussion – coping with difficult children | | ISSUE 3 |
| | Listening for gist | Writing a story<br>Dialogue preparation | | | ISSUE 3 |
| Reading for gist | Listening for the main points | | Research task – TV news programes | | ISSUE 3 |
| Reading for gist | Listening for information | Writing about the future | | Word stress – suffixes | ISSUE 4 |
| Intensive reading (gap fill) | Listening for information<br>Identifying expressions | | Role-play | | ISSUE 4 |
| Reading for gist | | Dialogue writing<br>Discussion essays | Role-play;<br>discussion – family friction | | ISSUE 4 |
| Reading for information | Listening for stress and syllable patterns | Research task – limericks | | Word stress, rhythm, and intonation patterns | ISSUE 4 |
| Intensive reading | Listening for information | Writing a story | Discussion – Walton's story | | ISSUE 5 |
| Reading for gist | Listening for information<br>Identifying expressions | | | | ISSUE 5 |
| | | Writing instructions and a report | Discussion – setting up an experiment | | ISSUE 5 |
| Reading for information | | Research task – cultural issues | Discussion – cultural issues | | ISSUE 5 |
| Intensive reading | Listening for gist and inference | Writing a letter to the Editor | Discussion – *Lord of the Flies* | Contrastive stress | ISSUE 6 |
| Intensive reading (gap fill) | Listening to confirm answers | Dialogue preparation | Guessing game | | ISSUE 6 |
| | Listening to complete a summary | Writing a letter of advice | | Word stress | ISSUE 6 |
| Reading for information | Listening for tone and intonation patterns | Research task – a leaflet on politeness | | | ISSUE 6 |

# LANGUAGE INPUT

| | Part | Page | Topic | Grammar | Function | Vocabulary |
|---|---|---|---|---|---|---|
| **ISSUE 7** | 1 | 62 | The art of getting hitched quick | *too/enough* Sequence of adjectives | | Words in context |
| | 2 | 64 | Are schools unfair to girls? | Modifying comparatives *than me* and *than I am* | Moans and groans | Words in context |
| | 3 | 66 | The way we are | | | Words to describe personality |
| | Over to you! | 68 | Games people play | | | Games |
| **ISSUE 8** | 1 | 70 | A friend in need … | Phrasal verbs | | Phrasal verbs related to relationships |
| | 2 | 72 | Music power | *make*, *let* and *allowed to* | Requesting and granting permission | Words in context |
| | 3 | 74 | A national game | Group nouns | | Words in context |
| | Language awareness | 76 | Advertising | | | |

**77–80 Grammar review Issues 7 and 8; Grammar practice; Wise up! – Listening**

| | Part | Page | Topic | Grammar | Function | Vocabulary |
|---|---|---|---|---|---|---|
| **ISSUE 9** | 1 | 82 | Worth a thousand words? | Third conditional | | Words in context |
| | 2 | 84 | If only … | Third conditional with present outcome *I wish/If only* + past perfect | Expressing regrets | Words in context |
| | 3 | 86 | Over-trained and under stress? | | | Sports |
| | Over to you! | 88 | Making a radio programme | | | |
| **ISSUE 10** | 1 | 90 | Signs of the times | *must, have to, mustn't, needn't, don't have to* | | Words in context |
| | 2 | 92 | If Mum could see me now! | *would rather* + base form or simple past *It's time* + simple past; *had better* | Giving advice | Words in context |
| | 3 | 94 | Ladies and gentlemen … | | | |
| | Language awareness | 96 | Pop | | | |

**97–100 Grammar review Issues 9 and 10; Grammar practice; Wise up! – Speaking**

| | Part | Page | Topic | Grammar | Function | Vocabulary |
|---|---|---|---|---|---|---|
| **ISSUE 11** | 1 | 102 | So much for romance | Reported speech | | Words in context |
| | 2 | 104 | The right to fight | Gerund and infinitive | Predicting | Words in context |
| | 3 | 106 | True stories | Adverbs of manner | | |
| | Over to you! | 108 | Poetry posters | | | |
| **ISSUE 12** | 1 | 110 | Eureka! | Relative clauses | | Words in context |
| | 2 | 112 | Home truths about TV | Participle clauses | Criticizing | Words in context TV words |
| | 3 | 114 | The place I grew up | | | Words describing buildings |
| | Language awareness | 116 | Language and gender | | | |

**117–121 Grammar review; Grammar practice; Wise up! – Writing**

# SKILLS DEVELOPMENT

| Reading | Listening | Writing | Speaking | Pronunciation | |
|---------|-----------|---------|----------|---------------|---|
| Reading for gist | Listening for information | | | used – /ju:st/ or /ju:zd/ | |
| Reading to assess style and to give an opinion | Identifying expressions | | Guided debate | | **ISSUE 7** |
| | Inference and listening for information | Writing descriptions | Discussion – appearance and attitudes | | |
| | | Research task – design a trail game | Discussion – board games | | |
| Reading for gist | | | Discussion – friendships | Sentence stress | |
| Intensive reading | Identifying expressions | Dialogue preparation | | | **ISSUE 8** |
| Reading for gist | | Describing an event | Discussion – similarities and differences | | |
| Reading for information | | Research task – analysing adverts | Matching adjectives to products | | |
| Intensive reading | Listening for information | Writing a story/description | | Word stress | |
| Scanning a text to confirm answers | Listening for information and expressions used | Summarizing | | | **ISSUE 9** |
| | Listening for information | Writing an opinion piece | Debate on whether sport can be harmful | | |
| | | | Research task – making a radio programme | | |
| Reading for the main points | | | Discussion – graphology | | |
| Intensive reading | Listening for information Identifying expressions | Dialogue preparation | | | **ISSUE 10** |
| | Listening for main points | Preparing a talk | Giving a short talk | Sentence stress | |
| Reading for information | Listening for information | Research task – a quiz on song lyrics | Discussion – song lyrics | | |
| Inference/reading for gist | | Writing a story | Discussion – 'dates' | Tone of voice | |
| | Listening for information Identifying expressions | | Discussion – boxing | | **ISSUE 11** |
| Reading for gist | Listening and giving an opinion | Using direct/indirect speech in narrative | | | |
| Reading poetry | | Research task – a poetry poster | | | |
| Intensive reading | Listening for information | | Role-play | Words ending in -ion | |
| Reading and summarizing | | Writing an opinion piece | Doing a class survey on TV habits | | **ISSUE 12** |
| Reading for gist | | Describing places | Debate | | |
| | | Research task – analysing magazines | Discussion – implied meanings | | |

Oxford University Press
Walton Street, Oxford OX2 6DP

Oxford New York
Athens Auckland Bangkok Bombay
Calcutta Cape Town Dar es Salaam Delhi
Florence Hong Kong Istanbul Karachi
Kuala Lumpur Madras Madrid Melbourne
Mexico City Nairobi Paris Singapore
Taipei Tokyo Toronto
and associated companies in
Berlin Ibadan

OXFORD and OXFORD ENGLISH
are trade marks of Oxford University Press

ISBN 0 19 432401 X

© Oxford University Press 1993

First published 1993
Fourth impression 1995

Set by Tradespools
Printed in Hong Kong

## Acknowledgements

*The publishers and author would like to thank the following for their kind
permission to use articles, extracts or adaptations from copyright material.
There might be instances where we have been unable to trace or contact the
copyright holder before our printing deadline. If notified, the publisher will
be pleased to rectify any errors or omissions at the earliest opportunity.*

Reader's Digest Magazine for *If Mum could see me now* by John Dyson,
*What price a cycle helmet?* by Liz Adlam, and *He just can't stop inventing*
by Peter Browne. Reader's Digest Association Limited 1990 for *Did you
know?* David Owen for *Best teacher I ever had*, adapted from Reader's
Digest Magazine; The Guardian for *Consumer Surveys* and *Alton Towers
Rescue*; The Times Saturday Review for *A Level English for mother and
teenager. Discuss*; Jonathan Cape and Curtis Brown Ltd, London, on
behalf of Heathcote Williams. Copyright © 1988 by Heathcote
Williams for *Whale Nation*; WH Allen – Virgin Publishing Ltd for *Just
the Job* by Rick Crowe; The sun Newspaper for *Luckiest man alive;* You
Magazine c/SOLO Syndication & Literary Agency for *Marriage
Japanese Style, Dr David Awesome Lawrence* and *Queen Charlotte
Richards*; HarperCollins publishers for *Between the Lines* by Richard
Brautigan from *Third Stages*; Eddison Sadd Editors Ltd for *The Best of
the Fortean Times*; Faber and Faber Ltd for *Lord of the Flies* by William
Golding; Collins Publishers – Fontana Book for *America – A User's
Guide* by Simon Hoggart; Sidgwick & Jackson for *Is that it?* by Bob
Geldof; Sony Music for *The times they are a-changin'* by Bob Dylan;
Penguin Books Ltd for *Love is... * by Adrian Henri from *The Mersey
Sound.*

*Illustrations by:*

Anna Brookes page 61; Richard Deverell pages 3, 80, 115; Nicki Elson
pages 21, 42, 69, 101; Belina Evans pages 33, 39, 53, 101, 102;
Gordon Hendry pages 34, 56, 68, 71, 88, 119; Ann Johns/Maggie
Mundy Illustrator's Agency pages 5, 27, 67, 78, 93, 98, 99; David
Loftus pages 16, 90; Debbie Lian Mason page 89; Colin Mier pages 14,
25, 84; Julie Morgan page 108; Alan Nanson page 72; Oxford
Illustrators pages 12, 44, 74, 87, 71, 74; Julie Tolliday pages 8, 29, 46,
47; Harry Venning pages 44, 51, 58, 73, 85, 96, 107, 111, 116

*Location photography by:*
Rob Judges

*The Publishers would like to thank the following for their permission to
reproduce photographs:*

Aquarius Picture Library page 113; All-Action Pictures page 49
(Duncan Raban – *Prince look-alikes*); Allsport pages 41 (Simon
Bruty – *swimmers*), 74 (J Daniel – *pitcher*), 81 (Simon Bruty –
*tennis coach*), 86 (Mike Hewitt – *tennis player*), 95 (Howard
Boylan), 105 (American football); Alpha Photographic Agency page
61 (Paul Harris – *wedding parlour*); The Ancient Art and
Architecture Collection page 41 (*Nazca lines*); Emily Anderson page
28; Anything Left Handed page 41 (*left handed products*); Arcaid
page 79 (Richard Bryant); Ardea pages 9 (Ron and Valerie Taylor –
*dolphin in net*), 12 (Nick Gordon – *Chinese river dolphin*), 19;
Barnaby's Picture Library page 68 (*backgammon*); Michael Brennan
page 101, 104 ('*Awesome' Lawrence*); Martyn Chillmaid pages 1
(*still life*), 29 (*teenagers*); Bruce Coleman Ltd pages 4 (Gerald Cubitt
– *rats*, Michael Waters – *grubs*), 5 (John Waters – *fish market*); Dr
Peter Collett pages 109/112 (*camera hidden in TV*); Colorific! pages
41 (Rob Crandall – *video game*), 48 (Patrick Ward – *Blackpool*), 49
(Alan Reininger – '*Marilyns*'); Coloursport page 75 (*cup final
match*); Philip Dunn pages 1 (*Japanese family*), 6, 29 (*old man/boy*);
The Environmental Picture Library page 5 (*dried seaweed*); The
Fortean Picture Library pages 41 (Frederick C Taylor – *crop circles*),
43; Ronald Grant Picture Library/The Cinema Museum pages 49
(*Lord of the Flies*), 50 ('*Piggy*'); Sally and Richard Greenhill Photo
Library page 61 (*science class*); Robert Harding Picture Library pages
21 (*fairground rides*), 68 (David Hughes – *snakes and ladders*), 109/
110 (Adam Woolfitt – *inventor*); Mark Harrison pages 9, 10
(*Marian and Katie Morris*); Impact Photo Library pages 4 (Roberta
Parkin – *egg*), 9 (Anthony Bindor – *dolphins*), 11 (Mark Cator – *old
man, UK*, Alain Le Garsmeur – *old man, Georgia*, John Cole – *old
woman*), 12 (Colin Jones – *Yangtze river*), 46 (Norman Lomax –
*motorbikes*), 48 (Brian Harris – *Ascot*, Philippe Achache – *Queen*),
62 (Alain Le Garsmeur – *Russian wedding*), 63 (Colin Jones –
*Bolivian wedding*, Homer Sykes – *Hindu wedding*), 68 (Rupert
Conant – *dominoes*), 81 (Cristophe Bluntzer – *cyclist*), 88 (John
Cole – *braille*), 109 (Homer Sykes – *tenement*, Alain Le Garsmeur –
*country house*), 114 (David Reed – *house, exterior*, Francois Perri –
*house, interior*); Life File pages 27 (Andy Teare), 48 (Miguel Arana –
*cricket*, Emma Lee – *feeding ducks*), 61 (Miguel Arana – *classroom*),
68 (Tim Fisher – *patience*, Andy Teare – *monopoly*), 69 (Emma Lee
– *baseball game*); The Kobal Collection page 50 ('*Ralph*')
Magnum Photo Library pages 68 (Sebastian Salgado – *chess*), 74
(Richard Kalvar – *candy floss*); Ander McIntyre pages 10 ('*Stephen
Frazer*'), 32, 96; Network Photo Library page 61 (Laurie Sparham –
*school gates*), 104 (Laurie Sparham – *boys boxing*); Operation Raleigh
Photo Library pages 89 (Dave Willis – *inflatable boat*), 92 (Dominic
Muscat and Dave Willis); Panos Pictures page 9 (Penny Tweedie –
*aboriginal man*); People Weekly © 1991 Marianne Barcellona page
30; Raymonds Press Agency page 22; Retna page 107 (Phil Loftus);
Frank Spooner/Gamma page 4 (*crickets*), 31 (*virtual reality*), 81
(*press*); Sporting Pictures UK pages 75 (*FA cup*), 86 (*swimmer*), 105
(*golfer*); Sygma pages 52 (Jacques Bourguey – *Queen look-alike*,
Mathiew Polak – *M Jackson look-alike*), 82 (Patrick Forester – *Liz
Taylor*); Tony Stone Worldwide Picture Library pages 61/62
(Thierry Cazabon – *Japanese wedding*); Trip Photo Library page 89
(Helene Rogers – *clinic*); John Walmsley Photo Library pages 46
(*skipping*), 48 (*milkman, gardening, dogs in park, eating chips*), 64;
Woman Magazine pages 21, 24 (*David Porter*)

*We would also like to thank the following for their help:*

Baxters of Speyside Ltd; Birmingham International Airport; Bryant
& May Ltd; CPC United Kingdom Ltd; Mr A Kamura and family,
OMRON, Telford Ltd; Roche Products Ltd

*The publishers would also like to thank the many ELT teachers around
the world who have given generously of their time to talk about their
needs, and to comment on Streetwise. Thanks are especially due to:*

*Leda Antoniou, Ralph Bannell, Rosa Borell, Denise Cripps, Costas
Gabrielatos, Frances Melling, Montserrat Riu, David Spencer, George
Vassilakis, Kate Wakeman, and Peta Xarhoulakou.*

# STREETWISE
## ISSUE 1

**SHOP TALK**

**FOOD GLORIOUS FOOD**

**YOURS**

Jogging in Hampton Park

# SHOP TALK

## WARM-UP

In Britain, personal questionnaires are a feature of most popular newspapers and magazines.

Are questionnaires popular in your country? Why/Why not? What kinds of topics do they cover? What do you think of questionnaires? Are they revealing or just a harmless form of entertainment?

## READING

Complete this questionnaire, then answer the questions that follow it.

### ARE YOU A TYPICAL TEENAGE CONSUMER?

Nobody is suggesting that you're all the same, but the marketing surveys that appear seem to think there are people out there who represent the youth of today. Is this true? Answer the following questions and find out.

**1  Are you fashion conscious?**
The magazines are full of the latest fashions. Do you go straight to the shops to try them on?

  **a** Yes. I always try my best to keep up with the latest styles.
  **b** I'm quite interested, but wouldn't say I was clothes mad.
  **c** No. Fashion doesn't interest me.

**2  Will you pay extra for designer clothes?**
You are in an exclusive boutique when you find some jeans that you really like. There's no price on them, but on your way to pay you decide that if they're over £50 you'll . . .

  **a** . . . have to put them back. There's no way you are going to spend that sort of cash on one pair of jeans.
  **b** . . . buy them without thinking twice. It's worth spending a bit extra for better quality.
  **c** You never go and pay if you don't know how much something is going to cost.

**3  How do you usually spend your cash?**
Someone has just given you a surprise gift of £30. What are you going to do with the money?

  **a** Go straight to the shops and buy something to wear.

  **b** Save it for later.
  **c** Buy some CDs or tapes.

**4  Are you brand conscious?**
Is there a difference between Pepsi Cola and Coca Cola?

  **a** No. Colas are all the same.
  **b** Yes, but I can't tell the difference!
  **c** Yes. I only drink the one I like.

**5  Are you an impulsive shopper?**
  **a** Yes. I love doing things without thinking about them.
  **b** No. I rarely act without thinking.
  **c** It depends. Sometimes I am, sometimes I'm not.

Market researchers suggest that today's 'typical' teenager will give the following answers:

**1** Teenagers are over twice as likely as the rest of the population to describe themselves as fashion conscious. The typical answer is a.

**2** Around one-third of teenagers said that they would spend at least £50 on one item of clothing without thinking. They're not in the majority though. The typical teenager does not have the money to worry about designer labels. The typical answer is a.

**3** Teenagers spend most of their money on clothes. This is followed by albums and CDs and going out. Saving comes well down the list. The typical answer is a.

**4** Teenagers are much more product conscious than adults. The typical answer is c.

**5** Most teenagers would describe themselves as impulsive. The typical answer is a.

**1** How many typical answers did *you* give?
**2** Use your own words to describe the view of a typical teenager as suggested by the questionnaire.
**3** Do you think that that there is such a thing as a typical teenager? Why/Why not?

## VOCABULARY

Find words and expressions in the text which mean:

*a*  young people of today
*b*  inform yourself about and buy clothes, etc.
*c*  expensive; limited to people who have a lot of money
*d*  without stopping to consider something
*e*  someone who is this does things suddenly and without thinking

---

*Glossary*

**marketing:** part of business that is concerned with how a product is sold, its price, etc. Market researchers help by providing information about products, what customers want, etc.

**brand:** particular make of goods, or their trade mark

**conscious:** aware. Used in expressions like 'politically conscious' to describe someone who believes that a particular aspect of life is important.

## Talking about the present

*a* What tense is used in these examples? Why?

*How do you spend your cash?*
*Teenagers spend lots of money on clothes.*

*b* Explain the difference between:
*I try to do my best.*
*I'm trying to do my best.*

*c* Some verbs are rarely found in the progressive form, e.g. *know*. Find as many examples as you can in the text.

*d* Find adverbs in the text that describe how frequently something happens and place them on this scale.

always ├────┼────┼────┤ never

## PRACTICE

1 Think about your shopping habits. Use adverbs of frequency and appropriate present-tense verbs to write a paragraph describing them. Summarize your attitude to shopping before answering questions such as *Who do you go with? Where? When? How often? What do you buy? Are you impulsive?*, etc.

Example
*I love going shopping. I usually go with my friend Marc...*

2 Work in pairs or small groups. Prepare a questionnaire about shopping habits. Try and find out what kinds of things people buy, where and when they shop, who they go with, etc. Try your questionnaire on another group and report the results.

## LISTENING 📼

A recent survey suggests that almost 60% of shoppers enter stores not knowing what they intend to buy, and of those, more than half buy on impulse. *Streetwise* reports on some of the ingenious ways supermarkets and chain-stores try to influence our shopping.

1 Look at the diagram of the inside of a supermarket. Identify the following.

*a* a trolley        *d* a freezer-cabinet
*b* a check-out      *e* a shelf
*c* an aisle         *f* a bakery

2 Some of the text is missing. Try and guess what is missing before listening to the tape to check your answers.

Bright lights make supermarkets seem ____ .
Supermarkets are laid out so that ____ .
This is why the entrance corridor ____ .
The purchase of items like bread, eggs, milk, etc., is pre-planned. These are placed ____ .
Most people stop buying when a basket is full so supermarkets ____ trolleys.
The ends of aisles are called ____ . Products here sell ____ .
Smells from the bakery encourage ____ .
Chocolates and sweets are often placed ____ so that parents buy them for bored children.

3 In what ways are supermarkets in your country similar or different?

## Improve your wordpower

Complete this grid and discuss your answers with the class. Use a dictionary to help.

|   |                  | Size            | Sells                          |
|---|------------------|-----------------|--------------------------------|
| *a* | supermarket    | large or small  | food, household goods, etc.    |
| *b* | kiosk          |                 |                                |
| *c* | department store |               |                                |
| *d* | market         |                 |                                |
| *e* | butcher's      |                 |                                |
| *f* | baker's        |                 |                                |
| *g* | greengrocer's  |                 |                                |
| *h* | chemist's      |                 |                                |
| *i* | newsagent's    |                 |                                |
| *j* | shopping mall  |                 |                                |

# FOOD GLORIOUS FOOD

## *WARM-UP*

One man's meat is another man's poison.
*Traditional proverb.*

A speciality at one of London's oldest and most famous restaurants is steak and oyster pie. Traditionally, this is accompanied by a glass of stout which is a strong dark beer. But members of four major world religions would find this meal repulsive. Hindus object to eating beef. Orthodox Jews do not eat shellfish. Muslims do not drink alcohol, and Buddhists do not eat meat at all. On the other hand, that same restaurant would not consider serving horsemeat. In Britain, horsemeat is only used for pet foods. In France, however, there are butcher's shops which specialize in horsemeat for human consumption.

All societies regard certain foods as untouchable or disgusting. Few North Americans or Europeans would look forward to a menu of ants, caterpillars, locusts, ducks' feet, thousand-year-old eggs, or bird's nest, but all are eaten every day somewhere in the world: ants in Latin America, Asia and Africa; caterpillars among Australian aborigines; locusts among the Navaho Indians in North America and in North Africa, and thousand-year-old eggs, ducks' feet, and bird's nest in China.

1 Make a list of foods mentioned.
  Which of these would be unappetizing to the majority of people in your country?
  Which of these would you like to try?
2 Decide what it is that makes certain foods unappetizing.

## *LISTENING* 😞

What would you do if you were offered bird's nest soup and thousand-year-old eggs? *Streetwise* reporter Andrea Lynch went to London's Chinatown to find out more.

1 Listen and complete these notes.

|  | Bird's nest | Thousand-year-old eggs |
|---|---|---|
| **What is it/are they?** | ____ | ____ |
| **Appearance** | looks like ____ | look like green ____ |
| **Taste** | tastes ____ | taste like ____ |

2 Why do people eat bird's nest?
3 Listen to the interviews again. Write down the expressions that people used to indicate that they did not like the look of what they were being offered.

## *VOCABULARY*

1 Work in pairs. Try and agree on a meaning for the phrases written here in *italic*.
a ... vegetables are often *boiled to death*.
b They've got *a lovely texture.* si sente con le mano
c 'Would you like to try this thousand-year-old egg?' '*You must be joking!*'
d Nobody was *keen on the idea* of trying one. VERY IN'
e They're rather nice. ... I think I could *develop a taste for* these.
f Next time friends from another country *turn their noses up* at what you offer ...

---

### *Improve your grammar*

**feel, look, seem, smell, sound, taste**

Verbs like *feel, look, seem, smell, sound* and *taste* can be used with adjectives.

Example
*The food tasted good.* (= The food was good to taste.)
NOT The food tasted well.

*Feel, look, seem, smell, sound* and *taste* can be followed by *like* + noun or *like* + adjective + noun.

Example
*It looks like (tiny) doughnuts.*

We do not usually use the progressive form with these verbs.

*It tastes horrible.*
NOT It is tasting horrible.

We can use the progressive form when *feel* and *look* express the physical or emotional state of a person.

*I'm feeling sick/nervous/disappointed/etc.*

## Improve your wordpower

1 Which do you think is the odd-one-out? Why?
a lamb beef chicken fish
b lettuce tomato aubergine courgette
c banana apple strawberry pear
d fry grill boil bake
e yoghurt cheese butter jam

2 Which of these adjectives best describes the foods on the cover? creamy, delicious, delicate, disgusting, sweet, hot, sour, bitter, salty, strong, tempting, juicy, rich, nasty.

## PRACTICE 1

1 What food do you hate most? Why? Use the structures in the *Improve your grammar* box to describe it. Read your description to the class and see if they can guess what you are describing.

2 Imagine that you were present when these photographs were taken. Work with a partner and list:
- the things you saw
- the sounds you heard
- the smells
- the colours, etc.

You are writing to a friend. Describe the market using an appropriate form of *look*, *smell*, *sound*, *seem* and *feel*.

Example
*The market was very busy. The food looked strange and unfamiliar . . .*

## Use and usage

### Questions with *like*

*What* + appropriate form of *be* + subject + *like?* is used to ask someone to describe the subject or give their opinion of it.

Example
*'What is your house like?' 'It's quite big.'*

But compare the following:
*'What is Kim like?'* (= describe Kim generally) *'She's intelligent and very nice to work with.'*
*'What does Kim look like?'* (= describe Kim physically) *'She's tall and slim.'*

Answer these questions.

1 What is your national dish like?
2 What does your best friend look like?

## GETTING STREETWISE! ☺

### Compliments

In Britain, people often compliment parents on their children.
It's also common to compliment people on bikes, cars, houses, etc.
It is also polite to compliment people if they have made something for you, like a meal.
However, you rarely compliment someone on something personal such as their hair, unless you know them well.

1 Look at the picture. Would a compliment be appropriate in this situation in your country? What would you say?

2 You are going to hear four extracts of people giving and receiving compliments. Listen and complete the table.

| | Situation | Expressions that helped me decide | Compliments used |
|---|---|---|---|
| 1 | | | |
| 2 | | | |
| 3 | | | |
| 4 | | | |

## PRACTICE 2 ☺

1 Listen and repeat with the appropriate intonation.
2 Work in pairs. Compliment your neighbour on as many things as you can.

# YOURS

## WARM-UP
Look at these extracts from letters.

1   How much can you tell about the people involved, from these extracts alone?

> Dear Marisa,
>
>    Many thanks for your last letter. I'm sorry that I haven't replied earlier but I've been terribly busy with my exams. Thank goodness they're over! Anyway, I'm really looking forward to seeing you when you come over to visit us next month.

> Dear Rob,
>
>    I've been here for just over a week and it's great. We have this fabulous room with a view of the beach and we spend most of our day . . .

2   Look at the extracts again. What are the writers trying to do in their opening sentences?

## READING
Read this letter from a Japanese girl to her American pen-friend and answer the questions.

32 Thames Court,
Victoria Avenue,
Hampton.
30 September 1991

Dear Margaret,

   I'm sorry I haven't written earlier but life has been very busy. We've been in England for about six months now and we are just beginning to settle in. I like living here. In Tokyo, Dad was never home before midnight. Here, he is usually home by eight or nine. He's a lot more relaxed because he has more free time and the family have started jogging together. He and I have even started playing golf!

Mum felt really miserable for the first few months but I think she's beginning to like it. Her English is improving and she has joined the local women's group. She is very popular and everybody talks to her because there are no other Japanese people in the village. Her women's group often goes to the theatre at night and she sometimes goes without my father! This is something she would never be able to do back home. They still don't like me going out alone but I'm working on it.

   Anyway, how's life been for you? I'd like to hear from you and I really am looking forward to my next exchange visit, but my main reason for writing is to see if you'd like to come and visit us during the Easter holidays. We'd love to see you. I do hope you can come.

   Give my regards to your Mum and Dad.

   Yours,
   Yoko

PS The enclosed picture was taken at my birthday party.

a   How has life changed for Yoko and her family?
b   At what point does Yoko change the subject? How does she signal the change?
c   What is the function of the exclamations and underlining?
d   When do we use the abbreviation PS?

## TALKING POINT
What are the most positive and negative aspects of life in your country? Would it be easy for someone like Yoko and her family to settle in? Why/Why not?

### Use and usage

#### Agreement
1   Decide if these subjects are singular or plural.
a   my mum and dad      e   nobody
b   the Japanese        f   everyone
c   a women's group     g   the news
d   each winner

2   Choose the correct form.
a   There *is/are* a lot of people outside.
b   There *was/were* nothing in the box.
c   There *is/are* some eggs in the box.
d   There *was/were* no news.

## Improve your writing

### Writing a personal letter

1  Put your own address in the top right-hand corner of the letter. You do not include the address of the person you are writing to in a personal letter.

2  These ways of writing the date are all acceptable.
*30th December 1993*
*30 December 1993*  *30/12/1993*
Put the date under your address.

3  Put a comma after the greeting.
*Dear Marisa,*

4  The first sentence or paragraph introduces the letter and, if necessary indicates the reason you are writing.
*It was great hearing from you again . . .*
*I thought I'd write to . . .*
*I'm sorry I haven't written . . .*

5  Use an appropriate style. Personal letters often include:
   - contractions (*I'm* not *I am*)
   - exclamation marks, underlining, etc., to make the letter more lively (*It's great!*)
   - words like *well* or *anyway* to signal a change of topic.

6  Round the letter off with a paragraph in which you 'take your leave'.
*(I) Hope to hear from you soon.*
*See you next week! (month/year/etc.)*

7  Sign off.
   - *Best wishes* or *Yours* can be used in most informal letters.
   - Use *Love* with close friends and relations.
   - Boys writing to other boys often end with *From* or just their name.
   - We normally use a comma after these expressions.
   - *Yours sincerely* and *Yours faithfully* are used in formal rather than personal letters.
   - When x is used after a letter is signed it indicates a kiss.

*Chris*
*xx*

## PRACTICE

1  Choose the appropriate form. Give reasons for your answer.

a  We have been on holiday for a week now. I *stay/am staying* in a small hotel. I *go/am going* swimming most afternoons and we usually *spend/are spending* the evenings at a disco. I *have/am having* a great time.

b  I *write/am writing* to see if you can come to a party at my house on 18 July. I have decided to celebrate my sixteenth birthday, and I *hope/am hoping* you will be able to come.

2  Use the prompts to write a complete letter.

a  Thank/for/letter which reach me/ Thursday.
*Thank you for your letter which reached me on Thursday.*

b  I be glad/hear you be well.

c  I just take/exams and I wait for/results.

d  My other news be that/start take dancing lessons.

e  They be great!

f  How about you? Do/still karate lessons, or you give up?

g  Anyway, I think I'd write/invite you/a party next month.

h  The invitation be enclosed.

i  /hope/can come.

j  Well,/must run. I be late/a private lesson.

k  See/soon.

## WRITING

Imagine Yoko's letter was addressed to you. Write a reply. In your reply you should:
   - Acknowledge her letter.
   - Give her the latest news about you and your family.
   - Talk about your recent activities, feelings, opinions, etc.
   - Respond to her invitation.
   - Bring the letter to a suitable conclusion.

Use as many of the words and expressions you have learnt in this issue as possible.

# Over to you!

## CONSUMER SURVEYS

### *READING*

### TESTING FOR THE BEST

Consumers need protection against the claims of advertisers. Some magazines and newspapers do this by publishing consumer reports on similar products. These can be the result of expert opinion or extensive tests. If you look at leaflets about sports shoes, you will find claims about their stability, weight, flexibility, and grip. Here are some ideas as to how you can test these claims yourselves.

#### *Weight*
Some sports shoes are said to be very light. Collect a number of different shoes of the same size and weigh them. How do sports shoes compare in weight to other footwear?

#### *Flexibility*
Shoes should be flexible to let the foot bend. Hold 15cm of the shoe with the heel on the edge of the table. Bend the shoe up and down as far as it will go. Place a sheet of paper next to the edge, mark a line for the table height and mark how far the shoes bend. You will then be able to compare the flexibility of various shoes of the same size.

#### *Stability*

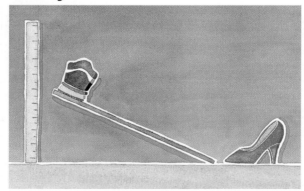

If you are running or jumping, it is important your shoes allow you to land without falling and injuring yourself. Place a shoe on a board. Raise the board at the shoe end 5cm at a time until the shoe falls over. Measure the angle at which this happens.

*1* Which of these features is most important in sports shoes for your favourite sport?

### *TALKING POINT*

Grip and the ability to absorb impact are also important qualities. Some shoes absorb the impact of the weight of your body as you walk or run, and contain springy material to help push your foot off into the next step. Most sports shoes have special soles to maximize grip, and if you look at the bottom of shoes you will notice that shoes have distinctive grip patterns.

*1* Work in pairs or small groups. Decide how you would test for the ability to absorb impact and grip using the things in the diagram.

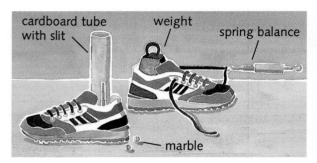

cardboard tube with slit — weight — spring balance — marble

### Research

*Aims:*
**1)** to decide on a product, and devise and carry out a consumer test of your own. (Work in pairs or small groups.)
**2)** to report on the test.

### *Hot tips!*

- Decide on the criteria for evaluating your product, e.g. taste and appearance may be important criteria for judging fruit drinks.
- Decide on how you are going to evaluate the product against the criteria you have chosen, e.g. you may wish to get people to taste a drink without knowing which one they are tasting. You may wish to combine interviews with tests.
- Decide on how you are going to present your results. Graphs or tables can be an efficient way of conveying information. If you use these, make sure that they are clear and have a title.

 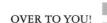

# STREETWISE
## ISSUE 2

## CLASS MATES!

## LAST CHANCE

A quarter of a million dolphins are killed annually by the tuna-fish industry...

On Mornington Island, in the Gulf of Carpentaria in Northern Australia, lives a tribe of Aborigines known as the Dolphin people. This tribe has been reported to be in direct communication with the wild bottlenose dolphins who reside just off the coast . . .

## DEAR SIR/MADAM

# CLASS MATES!

## WARM-UP

Marian Morris is 42. Earlier this year she went back to school to do A level English. She shared a classroom with her daughter Katie, and Stephen Frazer interviewed them about the experience.

Which of these statements belong to Marian? Which to Katie? Give reasons for your answers.

'If I go up to my bedroom and surround myself with books I think – Wow, I'm not doing the ironing or cleaning – this is my space.'

'Every time she opens her mouth I worry about what she's going to say and if she's going to make a fool of herself.'

'I've never felt embarrassed.'

'Every time she said something intelligent in class I wanted to clap.'

'The time she embarrassed me the most was when we were sitting in an exam working away and I smelled this funny smell. I looked over and she was pouring herself coffee.'

## LISTENING

Listen and check your predictions.

Now answer these questions.

1  Why did Marian go back to school?
2  How does Katie feel about it? Use what she says to support your opinion.

## VOCABULARY

1  Listen to the tape again, and explain the meaning of these phrases. Discuss your answers in pairs before using a dictionary.

a  a traffic jam
b  it only lasted a term
c  a mature person
d  gives me time off
e  that's worn off
f  I don't think I inhibit the girls
g  big enough to see

### Glossary

**A level:**
Advanced level;
exam taken at
the end of
secondary
school in the UK

## PRONUNCIATION
### Sentence stress

1  Listen to the tape again and underline the words which are given greater stress than usual in these examples.

Katie do you have to?

I hadn't got A for anything before and I got three per cent more than Mum ...

This is something for me, if I go up to my bedroom and surround myself with books I think – Wow, I'm not doing the ironing or the cleaning – this is my space.

2  Why were these words stressed more than others?

3  Listen and repeat with the same stress and intonation.

## Use and usage

### school or the school

With some nouns, we do not use *the* after a preposition when we're talking 'in general', or thinking about the main purpose of that building or other place.

*Marian went back to school last year.*
*She is coming out of hospital on Wednesday.*

We use *the* when we're talking about a specific building or place.

*The school is near the city centre.*
*There are 50 beds in the hospital.*

Decide if you need *the* in these examples.

a  My uncle is in _____ prison.
b  We went to _____ university, but the gates were locked.
c  She's a nurse at _____ local hospital.
d  Her husband went to _____ school to collect the children.

## Grammar quiz 1

### Present perfect

Look at these examples from the interview.

I *have worked* as a secretary for eighteen years ...
I'm older, *I've read* more books ...

Why does Marian use the present perfect?

## PRACTICE 1

*Marian is forty two. Her husband is a University professor. She has worked as a secretary for eighteen years, ...*

Write similar sentences about the life and achievements of someone you know.

Show your sentences to another student and be ready to answer any questions they may have. e.g. What did she do before she got married? How long have they been married?, etc.

### *Improve your wordpower*

A school leaving certificate (e.g. A levels)? A university degree? Practical training?

In your opinion, what qualifications, if any, do you need for these jobs?

author, secretary, doctor, carpenter, lorry driver, plumber, police officer, artist, business executive, bank clerk, TV star.

## TALKING POINT

A
I think we should always respect what older people say. After all, they've seen more, read more, done more. They have a lot to teach us.

B
I don't see why we should automatically respect older people. They may have been around longer, but many of them have been saying and doing the same things for years. They don't have much to say about the world today.

Which point of view do you share more? A or B? Why?

Do you think that older people change and adapt? Does it matter if they don't? Do you think more of them should behave like Marian's mother? Why/Why not?

### Present perfect simple and progressive

Answer the questions.

1 Which example gives a greater sense of something continuing?
 a They have said the same thing for years.
 b They have been saying the same thing for years.

2 Which example suggests that the activity is definitely over? Which example suggests that the activity may or may not be over?
 a Marian has done her homework.
 b Marian has been doing her homework.

3 Would you choose the simple or progressive form of the present perfect for these sentences. Why?
 There are books everywhere. They ____ (read) all morning. We ____ (read) four books so far this term.

4 When can you use the present perfect progressive rather than the present perfect simple?

## PRACTICE 2

Complete the following sentences with the present perfect simple or progressive. Give reasons for your choice.
 a She (study) all day.
 b Why is the pillow so wet? I think she (cry).
 c How long (you study) English?
 d Can I borrow your book? Sure, I (finish) it.
 e This book is very boring. I (only read) twenty pages this week!
 f What (you think) about?
 g I'm sorry. I (forget) your name.
 h The bus is very late. We (wait) for an hour.

## WRITING

Make the necessary changes and additions to Katie's description of herself.

My name/Katie Morris. I/seventeen. I go to The Green School in North London/three years. My subjects be A level Literature, Sociology, and Mathematics. For the last year/mother do A level Literature too. She be a good student. I think she read more books/me this term. I not mind have her my class, although she embarrass me/a number of occasions. The bad be when she start eat during/test. She work very hard so far, so I hope she get good marks/her exams.

# LAST CHANCE

## WARM-UP ☹

Listen to this extract from *Whale Nation* – a poetry and prose collection about whales and dolphins – and answer the questions below.

*a* Why was the killing of a dolphin punishable by death in ancient Greece?

*b* The poem suggests that this punishment might still be appropriate (*A punishment which may yet be on the books*). Share what you know about the ways in which dolphins have been mistreated in recent years.

## READING

Novelist Douglas Adams and zoologist Mark Cawardine went in search of disappearing wildlife, like the baiji dolphin which lives in the River Yangtze in China. Adams describes this as one of the 'biggest, longest, noisiest and dirtiest thoroughfares' in the world. In the bar of the Peace Hotel where a loud band is playing, Adams begins to understand why the dolphin has problems.

Share your ideas on the problems the baiji is likely to face before reading the text.

## BLIND PANIC ☹

Travelling in China I began to find that it was the sounds I was hearing that confused and disoriented me most.

It occurred to me, as we tried to find a table in one of the more muffled corners of the bar, that the dolphins we had come to look for must be suffering from the same kind of problem. Their senses must be completely overwhelmed and confused.

To begin with, the baiji dolphin is half blind.

The reason for this is that there is nothing much to see in the Yangtze. The water is so muddy now that visibility is not more than a few centimetres, and as a result the baiji's eyes have atrophied through disuse.

As a consequence, the baiji had to use a different sense to find its way around. It relies on sound. It has incredibly acute hearing and sees by echolocation, emitting sequences of tiny clicks and listening for the echoes. It also communicates with other baijis by making whistling noises.

### Glossary

**overwhelmed:** made to feel completely helpless

**echolocation:** seeing by the reflection of sounds

**clicks:** short, sharp sounds

**stroboscopic:** rapidly flashing bright light

**propeller:**

Since man invented the engine, the baiji's river world must have become a complete nightmare.

China has a pretty poor road system. It has railways, but they don't go everywhere, so the Yangtze (which in China is called the Chang Jiang, or 'Long River') is the country's main highway. It's crammed with boats the whole time, and always has been – but they used to be sailing boats. Now the river is constantly churned up by the engines of all sorts of ships.

I said to Mark, 'It must be continuous bedlam under the water.'

'What?'

'I said, it's hard enough for us to talk in here with this band going on, but it must be continuous bedlam under the water.'

'Is that what you've been sitting here thinking all this time?'

'Yes.'

'I thought you'd been quiet.'

'I was trying to imagine what it would be like to be a blind man trying to live in a discotheque. Or several competing discotheques.'

'Well, it's worse than that, isn't it?' Mark said. 'Dolphins rely on sound to see with.'

'All right, so it would be like a deaf man living in a discotheque.'

'Why?'

'All the stroboscopic lights and flares and mirrors and lasers and things. Completely confusing information. After a day or two you'd become completely bewildered and disoriented and start to fall over the furniture.

'Well, that's exactly what's happening, in fact. The dolphins are continually being hit by boats or mangled in their propellers or tangled in fishermen's nets.'

*a* Complete these notes to summarize the passage.

Baiji dolphins are half blind because ____ .
They rely on ____ to find their way.
The noise of ____ has affected the baijis' ability to find their way.
The result is ____ .
Adams compares this to ____ .

*b* What does the writer do to get us to understand the baiji's problem? Do you think he was successful? Why/Why not?

# VOCABULARY

What is the meaning of the words and expressions in **bold**?

a   the sounds **disoriented** me most
b   a more **muffled corner**
c   the baiji's eyes have **atrophied**
d   It has incredibly **acute** hearing
e   It's **crammed with** boats
f   it must be **continuous bedlam** under the water
g   you'd be **bewildered** and disoriented
h   **mangled** in the propellers
i   **tangled** in fishermen's nets

## Grammar quiz

Match the uses of the definite and zero articles to the examples.

### 1   Definite article

a   nothing diviner than the dolphin

i   with singular countable nouns when they stand for a species

b   in a discotheque where the ceiling

ii   with names of rivers, oceans or seas

c   the longest

iii   with the names of places that include *of*

d   the Yangtze

iv   when it is clear that there is only one

e   the Gulf of Carpentaria

v   with superlatives

### 2   Zero article

a   boats, Dolphins

i   Names of most towns, cities and countries except for The United States, the United Kingdom, etc.

b   China

ii   With plural countable nouns when making a general statement

c   to catch tuna

iii   with mass nouns when making a general statement

### 3   A/an

a   What is the difference between:
*Give me an apple.*
*Give me the apple.*

b   Would you use *a* or *an* for these words?
*apple, orange, banana, hour, holiday*
Other uses of the articles are on page 18.

# PRACTICE

Complete the following sentences with either *a/an*, *the*, or – (= zero).

a   Why are thousands of ____ dolphins dying?
b   ____ United States and ____ Canada have banned ____ drift nets from their waters.
c   It is wrong to keep ____ dolphins as ____ short-lived tourist attraction.
d   John Lilly wanted to make ____ film of ____ dolphin rescuing ____ human being in the water. His assistant pretended to be in distress, and ____ dolphin rescued him by pushing him to the side of the pool. Afterwards, Lilly found that ____ cap was still on ____ lens, so he took it off, and sent his assistant back into ____ water. When he pretended to be in distress again, ____ dolphin beat him up!
e   ____ whale oil is used for making ____ candles, ____ margarine, and ____ soap.

# PRONUNCIATION 😐
### the

When is *the* pronounced /ðiː/?
When is *the* pronounced /ðə/?

a   the EC
b   one of the more muffled corners
c   the environment
d   the air we breathe
e   the longest river

Listen and check your answers before repeating the phrases.

# GETTING STREETWISE! 😐
**Making and responding to suggestions**

A group of young people are discussing what they can do to help protect dolphins.

1   Listen and note down their ideas.
2   Write down the expressions they used to introduce the suggestions, and also the reactions to the suggestions. Decide if the reactions were positive, negative, or neutral.
3   Listen and repeat some of the suggestions and reactions.

# TALKING POINT

What is the main threat to endangered species like elephants, turtles, etc? What are the arguments for and against protecting animals?

Share your ideas with the class and suggest ways in which endangered animals could be given a last chance.

# DEAR SIR/MADAM

## READING

Read the advertisement on the cover of this issue and the reply below, before answering the questions.

Walnut Tree Cottage
School Lane
Foston
Lincs NG32 2IG

Personnel Department
European Patent Office
Erhardstrassa 27
Munchi

Meine Dame oder Heron,

   Pleas cosider me por the fost of typist what you want. I spotted youer ad in the Gradian today. I8m keen to get out of england and I8m told Munchi is a good place to hide be.

   I8m not bad at ptying as I8ve nearly finished my typing course at nightschool. I may need a dictionry though.

   Can you let me know as soon as possible whether I8m in the pictur because if I am I8ll finsh this typing course and save a few bob.

Yours faithfully,
Rick Crowe

The advertisement and letter are authentic. They come from a collection of letters published in a book entitled *Just the job!* The letters draw their humour from breaking the normal rules of letters of application. Work in pairs and answer these questions.

*a* What would a reply to such an advertisement normally contain?
*b* What is inappropriate about Crowe's letter?

### Glossary

**Gradian:** misspelling of *Guardian*, a leading English newspaper

**in the picture:** likely to be considered (very informal)

**a few bob:** a little bit of money (very informal)

## *Improve your writing*

### Writing a letter of application

*1* Make sure that you use an appropriate layout.
*2* Organize the content of your letter in the following way.

*a* **The introduction**
Use the first paragraph to state your reason for writing. If you are replying to an advertisement you should always mention where you saw it.
*I am writing in response to your advertisement in . . .*
*I wish to apply for the position of . . . which was advertised in . . .*

*b* **Main body of your letter**
Expand on your reason for writing. Draw attention to what makes you a particularly suitable applicant for the job/post, scholarship, course, etc.
Use present tenses to highlight your present situation/skills.
*I am X years old . . .*
*I'm going to be doing my school leaving exams in X years time . . .*
*I speak fluent German and good French.*
Use the present perfect/present perfect progressive to describe relevant recent or continuing experience:
*I have recently left school and I am a student at a Technical College where I have been doing a typing course . . .*
*I have used a word processor since I was thirteen.*
Use the past tense to describe relevant achievements in the past.
*When I was fourteen I was in the school quiz team.*
*When I was at school I worked on the school newspaper.*
Don't use contractions like *I'm, he's, they're* or informal expressions such as *Write soon* in formal letters.

*c* **Conclusion**
Conclude your letter. If appropriate state what you want or what you hope will happen next.
*I hope you will consider me for (the post, the scholarship, the course).*
*I look forward to hearing from you.*

## PRACTICE

**1** Complete the captions for the layout of a standard letter.

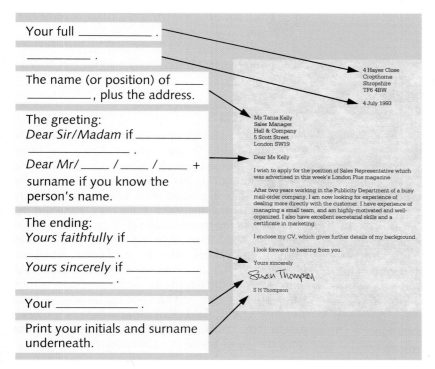

Your full _____ .

_____ .

The name (or position) of ____ _____ , plus the address.

The greeting:
*Dear Sir/Madam* if _____ _____ .

*Dear Mr/* ____ / ____ / ____ + surname if you know the person's name.

The ending:
*Yours faithfully* if _____ _____ .

*Yours sincerely* if _____ _____ .

Your _____ .

Print your initials and surname underneath.

*Letter shown in image:*

4 Hayes Close
Cropthorne
Shropshire
TF6 4BW

4 July 1993

Ms Tania Kelly
Sales Manager
Hall & Company
5 Scott Street
London SW19

Dear Ms Kelly

I wish to apply for the position of Sales Representative which was advertised in this week's London Plus magazine.

After two years working in the Publicity Department of a busy mail-order company, I am now looking for experience of dealing more directly with the customer. I have experience of managing a small team, and am highly-motivated and well-organized. I also have excellent secretarial skills and a certificate in marketing.

I enclose my CV, which gives further details of my background.

I look forward to hearing from you.

Yours sincerely

*Susan Thompson*

S H Thompson

**2** Use the prompts to write a complete letter in reply to this advertisement.

Young person with musical skills required to assist on nationwide summer courses for 6 to 8 year olds.
No experience required.
Write to . . .

Dear Sir
I see your advertisement/Issue 2 of *Streetwise*/write in/hope that you consider me for/job as a course assistant this summer.
I be 17 and study for/school leaving exams.
I play/piano for seven years and recently pass my advanced exams.
I always love children, and last year I look after two children/a month.
I not have any experience of working/a course, but I help in my uncle's shop since I be sixteen, so I be reliable and hard-working.
I always want to work with children, and I be very happy/join your team.
I look forward/hear from you.
Yours faithfully

**3** Work in pairs. Rewrite Rick Crowe's letter, inventing any additional details that are required.

## TALKING POINT 1

Work in small groups.

**1** Talk about what people do in three of these jobs.

| | |
|---|---|
| a computer operator | a disc jockey |
| a model | a police officer |
| a salesperson | an engineer |
| an air hostess | a hospital doctor |

**2** Advertisements for jobs often list the qualities of the kind of person they are looking for. For example:

experienced   enthusiastic   sociable
hard-working   highly motivated
numerate   honest   skilled   confident
caring   flexible   talented   innovative

Make sure you know what each of these mean. Can you add any more?

**3** Your teacher will give you two jobs. In your group decide on the five most important qualities needed for each one.

## WRITING

Write your own letter of application for this scholarship. Invent any details required.

---

**It's a Small World!**

*Small World* is an international charity that offers young people a chance to live and study in a country of their choice.

Apply for your scholarship now! Tell us about yourself and give us some idea of what you want to do and why.

If your letter is chosen, we will invite you to an interview and discuss your application further.

*Write to:* Mike Swallow, International Scholarships, Small World, World House, Trafalgar Square, London W1X

---

## TALKING POINT 2

Work in groups of three or four. Take it in turns to interview each other for the scholarship. As preparation you should read the letters of application and formulate appropriate questions such as:

*Why are you interested in . . . ?*
*Have you ever . . . ?*
*How long have you been . . . ?*

Remember the objective of an interview is to get candidates to talk and show what they are capable of, so avoid asking questions that are impossible to answer.

# OUR VIEW OF THE WORLD

## READING

Our view of the world is reflected in the expressions we use. Read the text and answer the questions.

### TIME IS MONEY

In British and American culture, time is seen as a valuable commodity. It is limited, and has to be used carefully to accomplish our goals. For example, work is typically associated with the time it takes and people are paid by the hour, week, or year. It is a culture where TIME IS MONEY in many ways: hourly wages, hotel room rates, interest on loans, etc. There are cultures where time is viewed quite differently, but look at these examples to see how the link between *time* and *money* is reflected in the English language:

How do you *spend* your time these days?
You're *wasting* my time.
This gadget will *save* you hours.
How much time can you *give* me?
That flat tyre *cost* me an hour.
I've *invested* a lot of time in this idea.
Is that *worth* doing?
He is living on *borrowed* time.
I *lost* a lot of time when I got sick.

1 How would you translate the expressions in the list? Do you have similar expressions in your language?

### EXPRESSIONS WITH TIME

Look at any major English dictionary and you will see the importance of *time* and how this is reflected in the large number of expressions containing this word.

2 Match the definitions (*i–vi*) to the expressions in *italics* (*a–f*).

*i* old-fashioned
*ii* had ideas that were too advanced for the period he lived in
*iii* before the period you can remember or are/were involved in
*iv* have nothing to do
*v* this is something that should have happened some time ago
*vi* early or with time to spare

*a* Alan is playing in the team this week; *and about time too*.
*b* Someone like Salvador Dali *was ahead of his time*.
*c* The Beatles were a bit *before my time*.
*d* The coat he is wearing is a little *behind the times*.
*e* I'm in no hurry. *I have time to kill*.
*f* There wasn't much traffic so we got there *in good time*.

## PROVERBS

Proverbs are short well-known sayings that state a general truth or give advice. They are often based on images which reflect our culture and view of the world. For example, many houses in England have a garden with a lawn. As a result, the expression *The grass is always greener on the other side of the fence* means that people are never satisfied with their own situation, and always think that others are in a better position. Moroccan Arabic has the same idea but expresses it differently in an expression which translates as *The neighbour's apples always taste sweeter*. The proverb *Half a loaf is better than none* exists in both languages, reflecting the importance of bread in both cultures.

3 Look at these English proverbs. For each proverb you should decide if your language:

*a* has almost exactly the same proverb.
*b* expresses the same idea but in different words.
*c* does not have the same idea at all.

Don't put all your eggs in one basket.
Don't cry over spilt milk.
Kill two birds with one stone.
A bird in the hand is worth two in the bush.
When the cat's away, the mice will play.
People who live in glass houses shouldn't throw stones.

### Research

*Aims:*

**1)** to make a list of ten of the most common proverbs in your language and, in English, explain what these mean.
**2)** to explain the extent to which you think these expressions reflect life in your country.
**3)** to find the English equivalents (if any).

# GRAMMAR REVIEW ISSUES 1 AND 2

## PRESENT TENSES

In English, we can use the simple present and the present progressive to talk about the present.

| Uses | Examples |
|------|----------|
| 1 Simple present: for something which happens regularly, or to talk about habits. | *He works in an office.* *I often chew my nails.* |
| 2 Simple present: to express a present state or general truths. | *I'm hungry.* *Do you like Beethoven?* *The sun rises in the east.* |
| 3 Simple present: to describe present events in commentaries, demonstrations, etc. | *Erik passes the ball to Anderson, who shoots...* *You beat the eggs and add them slowly...* |
| 4 Present progressive: to talk about events happening now. | *I'm washing my hair.* *It's raining.* |
| 5 Present progressive: to talk about a temporary habit. Use *always* to show annoyance. | *I'm learning English.* *She's always speaking on the phone.* |

### Notes

We can also use present tenses to tell stories or jokes. This has the effect of making them more lively.

*A woman is walking home. Suddenly she sees...*

For present tenses with future meaning (see page 37).

## NON-PROGRESSIVE VERBS

Some verbs are not normally found in progressive forms. These generally express a state rather than an action:

a   verbs of feelings/emotions, e.g. *like, love, hate*
    *I like going to the cinema.*
b   verbs of perception, e.g. *feel, hear, smell, see*
    *That smells nice.*
c   verbs of opinion, e.g. *think, know, appear, seem*
    *I think you are wrong.*   *I know her very well.*

### Note

Some of the verbs listed can be used in progressive forms when they are used with a different meaning. Compare:

*She thinks you are right.* (= opinion)
*She's thinking about it.* (= trying to make a decision)

## ADVERBS OF FREQUENCY

These answer the question *How often...?*

– *always* (i.e. all the time)
– *almost always, nearly always*
– *generally, normally, regularly, usually*
– *frequently, often*
– *sometimes, occasionally*
– *almost never, hardly ever, rarely, seldom*
– *not...ever, never* (i.e. none of the time)

Adverbs of frequency usually go before the main verb.

*I often feel hungry in the afternoon.*

## VERBS OF PERCEPTION

### Uses

1   Verbs like *feel, look, seem, smell, sound* and *taste* can be used with adjectives.

    *The food tasted good.* (= The food had a nice taste.)
    *That looks very nice.*

2   *Feel, look, seem, smell, sound* and *taste* can be followed by *like* + noun (or adjective + noun).

    *She sounds like Madonna.*

### Note

When they express a continuing perception we do not use the progressive form.

*It tastes horrible.* (NOT *It is tasting horrible.*)

When *feel* and *look* express the physical state of a person we can use the progressive.

*I'm feeling sick/nervous/disappointed/etc.*

## PRESENT PERFECT

The present perfect links the past and the present.

| Uses | Examples |
|------|----------|
| 1 For actions which began in the past and still take place or are happening now. | *She has worked as a secretary for ages.* *I have lived here all my life.* |
| 2 To relate experience (from the past up till now). | *Have you ever been to the disco? I've never seen you there.* |

### Note

A sentence like *I've seen this film* refers to a past action, but the time of the action is unspecified. If you want to specify the time of the past action you must use the simple past – *I saw this film last week.*

## PRESENT PERFECT SIMPLE AND PROGRESSIVE

1  We use the present perfect progressive to emphasise the duration of an action (i.e. how long).

*I've been doing this all morning.*

We use the present perfect simple to talk about what has been achieved (i.e. finished) in a period of time.

*I've done two exercises this morning.*

2  When we use the present perfect progressive, the action may or may not be finished. The emphasis is on the action.

*I've been cleaning my guitar.*

When we use the present perfect simple the action is finished. The emphasis is on the result.

*I've cleaned my guitar.*

### Note

With the verbs *work* (= have a job) and *live* you can use either form with little difference in meaning.

*He has lived/has been living here for years.*

## INDEFINITE ARTICLE (A/AN)

| Uses | Examples |
|---|---|
| With singular countable nouns: | |
| 1  for a general meaning (meaning 'any, it does not matter which'). | *Give me an eraser.* |
| 2  with a noun mentioned for the first time. | *There was a dog outside. The dog was very large.* |
| 3  with numbers (e.g. *a hundred*) and fractions (e.g. *a quarter*). | *There were a million people in Trafalgar Square.* |
| 4  to describe somebody's job or situation. | *My uncle is a doctor. My grandmother is a pensioner.* |

### Note

*an* is used before a word that begins with a vowel sound. Compare *an hour* /ən ˈaʊə(r) / and *a house* /ə ˈhaʊs/, *an MP* /ən ˌemˈpiː/ and *a mouse* /ə ˈmaʊs/, *an umbrella* /ən ʌmˈbrelə/ and *a university* /ə ˌjuːnɪˈvɜːsətɪ/.

### Pronunciation

*a* is usually pronounced /ə/.
*an* is usually pronounced /ən/.

## DEFINITE ARTICLE (THE)

*The* can combine with singular countable, plural countable, and uncountable nouns.

| Uses | Examples |
|---|---|
| 1  With singular countable nouns when they are an invention or species. | *The dolphin is an endangered species. He invented the telephone.* |
| 2  With names of rivers, oceans or seas. | *The Baiji live in the Yangtze.* |
| 3  With the names of places that have *of*. | *I went to visit the Tower of London.* |
| 4  When it is clear that there is only one. | *'Who's that at the door?' 'It's the postman.' Ann is in the garden.* |
| 5  With superlatives. | *She's the best!* |
| 6  With certain time expressions. | *I'll see you in the morning.* |
| 7  With a unique object or group of people. | *The earth is round. The Jacksons are great.* |
| 8  With a noun that becomes definite by being mentioned a second time. | *He stole a car. The car he stole was a Rolls Royce.* |

### Pronunciation

*The* is pronounced /ðə/ before consonant sounds and /ðiː/ before vowel sounds.

We can draw attention to a noun by using /ðiː/ to mean the one and only, or the main one.

*He is the person to speak to.*

## ZERO ARTICLE

In some cases no article is necessary.

| Uses | Examples |
|---|---|
| 1  With names of towns, cities and countries. | *Canberra is the capital of Australia.* |
| 2  With plural countable nouns when making a general statement. | *Dolphins and whales are mammals.* |
| 3  With uncountable nouns when making a general statement. | *Oil is a very important resource.* |
| 4  With names of meals. | *Breakfast is served.* |

### Note

The exceptions to point 1 above include countries whose names include nouns like *Republic*, e.g. *the United Kingdom*, *the Irish Republic*, and plural forms such as *the United States*, *the Canary Islands*.

# GRAMMAR PRACTICE

## A

**1** Complete the sentences with the simple present or the present progressive form of the verb in brackets.

Example

I *am doing* (do) my homework. Can you answer the door?

a 'Where's Alan' 'He _____ (sleep)'.
b It never _____ (rain) in August.
c What _____ he _____ (do)? I can't see him.
d I normally _____ (go) to work at this time.
e She _____ always _____ (pull) my hair.
f Please make the tea. The water _____ (boil).
g _____ you _____ (understand) him?

**2** Read this interview with an English teacher and choose the correct form.

a A How long *have you been/were you* teaching at this school?
b B *I've been here/I am here* for four years.
c A I see. Where were you before that?
   B I *worked/have worked* in a school in Spain.
d A Really? How long *have you been/were you* in Spain?
e B About three years. I *liked/have liked* it but I *decided/have decided* to move to a better job.

**3** Complete the sentences with *a/an*, *the*, or zero (–).

a What time do you go to _____ work?
b Do you often lie in _____ sun?
c Who is _____ best singer in _____ world?
d There were two people in the room, _____ man and _____ woman.
e Last year I visited _____ China and _____ India.
f What do you have for _____ lunch?
g Have you ever seen _____ elephant in the wild?
h Why is _____ letter E lazy?
   Because it is always in _____ bed!

## B

**1** Complete the dialogue.

A What is your favourite breakfast food?
B Rice crispies.
A What _____ like? (*a*)
B They're made from grains of rice.
A Ugh! That sounds _____ . (*b*)
B They're not! They're nice and crisp.
A What do they _____ ? (*c*)
B They don't have a strong taste. You need to add milk and sugar. When you do they make a noise.
A What does _____ ? (*d*)
B It's a popping sound.
A How _____ (*e*) eat them?
B Everyday!
A You must like them.
B I do. _____ (*f*) great when I eat them.

**2** Complete the sentences with the present perfect simple or progressive. Give reasons for your answers.

a He's a good friend. I _____ (know) him for years.
b Who _____ (eat) my sweets? The packet is almost empty.
c 'What's up?' 'I _____ (lose) my keys.'
d He _____ (do) karate for years.
e Bill _____ (leave) his old job. He _____ (work) in the United States for about three weeks now.
f I'm afraid I can't play. I _____ (broke) my leg.

**3** Complete the text with either *a/an*, *the*, or zero (–).

**Panda facts**
There are probably less than 1,000 wild pandas left in _____ (*a*) China. _____ (*b*) pandas used to be hunted, but that's been stopped. _____ (*c*) Chinese government has set up twelve special areas for _____ (*d*) pandas but their numbers are still falling. In _____ (*e*) 1980 _____ (*f*) World Wildlife Fund and _____ (*g*) People's Republic of China started _____ (*h*) project to learn more about _____ (*i*) giant panda. _____ (*j*) project was run by Western and Chinese scientists and they helped supply _____ (*k*) information to raise _____ (*l*) pandas in _____ (*m*) zoos outside _____ (*n*) China. A few years later _____ (*o*) baby panda was born in Madrid Zoo.

## C

**1** Write a short description of the sounds, smells, tastes and sights that you associate with a trip or journey that you make regularly. (e.g. a regular visit to the countryside, the trip to and from school, etc.) Use mainly present tenses.

**2** Write fifteen questions that you would like to ask one of your teachers about their career, life and interests.

# Wise up!

# VOCABULARY

## STORING VOCABULARY

It is very important that you find a way of building up your vocabulary.

1   Complete this questionnaire individually.

a   Do you record new words and phrases?
b   Do you use a vocabulary notebook? cards? something else (please specify)?
c   How do you organize the words?
  - Are they in alphabetical order?
  - Do you have a separate page for words that belong to a topic?
  - Something else (please specify)?
d   Do you have an explanation and examples for each word?
e   Are the explanations in English or your own language?
f   Do you include additional information about words, e.g. grammar, when they are used, etc?
g   How often do you review the words you have learnt in class?
h   Do you have a method of learning the spelling and meaning of new words, e.g. setting yourself quizzes, copying, etc?

2   Discuss your answers with other students. Find out if anyone else uses the same methods as you. Could you learn better using their method? Could you adapt it or improve on it? Remember it is important to experiment and choose a system that suits you and the way you like to learn.

## USING A DICTIONARY

A good learner's dictionary normally includes:

a   a clear definition of the word
b   information about the part of speech (e.g. n = noun, adj = adjective)
c   information about where a word can be divided, if necessary, when writing or typing
d   help with the stress and pronunciation
e   alternative spellings of the word (if any)
f   special information on grammar and how the word can be used
g   examples of different uses
h   explanations of idioms and phrasal verbs related to the word
i   alternatives in British and American English
j   information about opposites

1   Look at this entry from a dictionary.

sth): *It makes no difference to us if the baby is a girl or a boy.*
☆ **different** /ˈdɪfrənt/ *adj* **1 different (from/to sb/sth)** not the same: *Cricket is quite different from baseball.* ○ *The play was different to anything I had seen before.* ○ *The two houses are very different in style.* ☛ In US English **different than** is also used. **2** separate; individual: *This coat is available in three different colours.* —**differently** *adv*: *I think you'll feel differently about it tomorrow.*
**differentiate** /ˌdɪfəˈrenʃieɪt/ *verb* **1** [I,T]
**1 B**

*from the Oxford Wordpower Dictionary*

a   What information is provided?
b   Compare this entry to one for the same word in another dictionary.

## WHAT THE EXAMINER WANTS

In an exam, your knowledge of words and expressions may be tested directly. Here are some examples of typical exam questions:

  - Find words in the text that mean the same as the words in a list.
  - Write the opposite.
  - Choose the word or phrase which best completes a sentence, e.g.
    *My brother had his camera ____ from his car in the office car-park.*
    *A robbed   B missed   C lost   D stolen*

Vocabulary is also tested indirectly, because your knowledge of words will affect your performance in other papers, e.g. writing.

1   Find out if, and how, vocabulary is going to be tested in any exam you may be going to take.

## REVISING VOCABULARY

  - If possible, look through past papers to see what topics you are likely to meet in your exam. Build up your vocabulary in these topic areas.
  - Use common words such as *believe* to see if you can build up word families.

| Noun | Verb | Adjective | Adverbs |
|---|---|---|---|
| *belief* *believer* | *believe* | *believable* | *believably* |

1   Work in small groups and decide which of these strategies is most appropriate for successful vocabulary revision.

a   I learn long lists of words.
b   I revise for about two hours at a time.
c   I do a little revision each day.
d   I try and learn words in useful groups.
e   I revise about once a week.

# ISSUE 3

RESCUE

BRITAIN'S NAUGHTIEST CHILD?

BETWEEN THE LINES

# RESCUE

## *WARM-UP*

What is happening in the photographs?
What do they have in common with the ones
on the cover?
Do you think fun-fair rides are dangerous?
Why/Why not?
How would you feel if you had to be rescued in
this way?
Share your answers with the class.

## *READING*

1   Read one of the of the texts as quickly as
    possible to find the answers to these
    questions.
*a*   Where and when did the problem occur?
*b*   How were the people rescued?

### ALTON TOWERS RESCUE

A woman escaped by rope from a cable car stranded
over a 30m ravine at the Alton Towers leisure
complex yesterday.

She was among 28 people who were rescued from
three cars after the one in which she was riding
became tangled with a communications cable in
high winds. A computerised safety system halted the
40-car Sky Ride, and some passengers were trapped
for more than two hours.

The emergency services practised the same
rescue at Alton Towers two weeks ago, with staff
acting as trapped passengers.

A man in a wheelchair was lowered to safety by
firemen, who dropped a rope to the ground after
getting to the car with special equipment.

*From The Guardian*

### 27 SAVED IN MID-AIR DRAMA
### SKYRIDE TO TERROR

#### *Cable car traps trippers*

The thrill of the fair turned to horror for 27 Easter
trippers on a skyride yesterday.

Terrified passengers were stranded in mid-air
above a 30m ravine for an agonizing two hours after
their cable cars had come to a halt at Britain's
biggest amusement park.

A small child who clung desperately to his rescuer
was among the frightened holidaymakers who had
to be lowered by ropes in the strong winds.

His mother broke down in tears as they were
reunited in the ambulance taking them from Alton
Towers, Staffordshire.

Rescue hero Mark Symonds had to crawl along
the cable to reach the cars. He battled with the high
winds to climb down a ladder into the stranded cable
car.

Mark, 25, said afterwards: "The people inside
were obviously very relieved to see me."

One weeping girl said: "I thought we'd never get
down. I kept thinking we're going to die."

*From The Daily Mirror*

Now answer the questions.

1   Use information in the articles to explain
    why the cable cars stopped and how the
    passengers were rescued.
2   What are the factual differences between the
    two reports?
3   *The Guardian* is a 'quality' newspaper. *The
    Daily Mirror* is a 'popular' one. Compare
    the two reports. Consider:
    ■   the length
    ■   the vocabulary used (*terrified, horror,*
        etc.)
    ■   the information that is included or
        excluded
    ■   the order in which the information is
        presented (For example, is the story told
        in the order in which it happened? Why/
        Why not?)

---

**Glossary**

**ravine:** very
deep, narrow,
steep-sided
valley between
hills or
mountains

**the emergency
services:** the fire
brigade, police,
ambulance, etc.

---

# VOCABULARY

1 Match the words and expressions in column A to the explanations in B. Not all the expressions have explanations. Write explanations for the remaining ones.

| | A | B |
|---|---|---|
| *a* | tangled | take people away from danger |
| *b* | thrill | very worrying |
| *c* | stranded | |
| *d* | agonizing | crying |
| *e* | had come to a halt | feeling of excitement and pleasure |
| *f* | clung desperately | left in a difficult situation, unable to escape |
| *g* | high winds | |
| *h* | battled | twisted in an untidy way |
| *i* | weeping | fought |
| *j* | rescue | |

# PRONUNCIATION ☻

## Reading aloud

1 Read silently as you listen to a reading of part of the text from *The Daily Mirror*.

2 Listen to the same passage broken up into short phrases. Try and repeat what you hear with the same word-linking and intonation.

## Grammar quiz

### Past tenses

1 Look through the texts and find examples of the following:

   *a* an irregular simple past
   *b* the past progressive
   *c* the past perfect
   *e* the past passive

2 When do we use the past perfect rather than the simple past?

3 When do we use the past progressive rather than the simple past?

4 Why is the passive often used in news reports?

# PRACTICE

1 Complete this news report by putting in the missing verbs in an appropriate tense.
   be   be   say   step   miss   recover
   survive   smash   explode   drive   crash
   be taken   be broken

## LUCKIEST MAN ALIVE

Jet disaster survivor Pierre Lota ＿＿＿ the luckiest man alive this morning.

   The 45-year-old businessman ＿＿＿ unhurt from the wreck of an airbus just five hours after he ＿＿＿ his car on a French motorway.

   A crash expert ＿＿＿ : 'He must be the luckiest man on earth. He ＿＿＿ from his car crash when the plane went down.' Mr Lota ＿＿＿ one of nine people who ＿＿＿ when Air Inter Flight IT 5148 crashed into a mountain and ＿＿＿ five minutes from landing.

   He ＿＿＿ to Lyon on Monday to catch an earlier flight when his car left the motorway. He ＿＿＿ to hospital but the x-rays showed no bones ＿＿＿ and he continued his journey.

   When he reached Lyon airport, he knew he ＿＿＿ his flight but he boarded Flight 5148 instead. Fifty-five minutes later the plane ＿＿＿ into the side of a mountain.

## Improve your wordpower

1 Which of these disasters is natural? Which ones can be the result of human error?

   *earthquake, plane crash, famine, flood, drought, shipwreck, hurricanes*

2 The aftermath of major disasters normally follows a pattern. In what order would these events normally occur?

   *organising relief supplies*
   *first aid at the scene*
   *a search for survivors*
   *evacuation of the seriously injured*
   *an investigation into the causes*

# WRITING

1 Imagine you were one of the people at Alton towers. Write and tell your story to the *It happened to me* column of *Streetwise*.

# BRITAIN'S NAUGHTIEST CHILD?

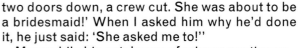

## *WARM-UP*

Do you know any young children who are very naughty? What are some of the worst things they have done?

## *READING*

Read this article about Britain's naughtiest child and see how he compares to the people you have been talking about.

### WATCH OUT, DAVID'S ABOUT!

David Guest was just two and a half years old when he climbed into the family car and bumped it down the road in second gear. He was five when he set fire to his mum's bedroom.

His mother, Marlene, is in despair. Her seven-year-old 'Dennis the Menace' has an angelic face, wavy gold hair, blue eyes, a gap-toothed grin, and long thin legs covered with bruises. The afternoon I visited the family's home was just a normal, dreadful 'David day'.

Trying to be good – he always tries to be good, he just forgets what bad is – he runs upstairs to get a book. There is a huge crash and then silence. 'See what I mean?' says Marlene.

In the bedroom a total mess greets us. David is on the floor, wriggling out of a wardrobe full of books and toys. He has pulled it over climbing up to the top shelf – 'I was just trying to get something'.

Usually, his problems are caused by curiosity. He loves taking things apart but cannot always put them back.

His worst crime to date was the bedroom fire. Marlene remembers, 'I was about to go to bed when I noticed a funny smell coming from my room. When I went upstairs I found that my bed was on fire. I had to call the fire brigade.'

'We took David to Paris with us and one of the things I've always wanted to do was to visit the Cathedral of Notre Dame. But just as we were about to go inside, David ran away. I thought we'd seen the last of him. Eventually two police officers brought him back. And after all that I never got to see Notre Dame.'

Surprisingly, David doesn't often get into trouble at school because he's rarely bored, but the neighbours often suffer when the lessons are over. 'Once he gave a little girl of four, who lives

*Glossary*

**Dennis the Menace:** young, male, cartoon character who is lovable but very naughty

**gap-toothed:** having teeth which are wide apart

**crew cut:** a very short hair style for men as worn by people working on a ship (the crew)

two doors down, a crew cut. She was about to be a bridesmaid!' When I asked him why he'd done it, he just said: 'She asked me to!'

Meanwhile his catalogue of crimes continues.

Now answer the questions.

1. Does David look naughty or not?
2. What did he do while the reporter was talking to his mum?
3. Did David's mother get to visit Notre Dame? Why/Why not?
4. In your opinion, which was the worst 'crime' mentioned in the text?
5. Why do you think he is so naughty?

## *VOCABULARY*

What is the meaning of these words and phrases from the text?

| | | | |
|---|---|---|---|
| a | grin | d | curiosity |
| b | dreadful | e | take a thing apart |
| c | wriggling | f | to date |

## *Improve your grammar*

### Future in the past

The future in the past can be expressed by *was going to, was about to, was on the point of.*

1. These forms can refer to events which were planned to take place, and which did take place.

   *He gave a little girl a crew cut. She was about to be a bridesmaid.*

2. They can refer to events which were intended, but which did not happen at the time because something interrupted or prevented them.

   *But just as we were about to go inside the Cathedral, David ran away . . . (so we didn't go inside).*

3. *Was about to* and *was on the point of* both carry the suggestion that the 'future in the past' event was very near.

   *It was 8.59 and the lesson was on the point of starting when he walked in.*

In sentences like *I was going to see him* or *I was about to see him* we need further information to know whether the meeting took place or was prevented.

# PRACTICE

**1** Use *was about to* and *was going to* to make sentences about each of the situations.

Example
*They were about to enter Notre Dame when David ran away.*

**2** Imagine that you were also very naughty when you were younger. Use the structures in the *Improve your grammar* box to write five sentences about some of the things you were going to do when you were interrupted.

*I think he's . . .*

## Improve your wordpower

**1** What is the meaning of the expressions in **bold**?

**a** We always **make up** after arguing.
  *i* use cosmetics
  *ii* become friends again

**b** I used to **get away with** a lot because I was the youngest child.
  *i* steal
  *ii* escape unpunished

**c** My father used to punish me but my mum often used to **let** me **off**.
  *i* not oblige someone to do something
  *ii* give someone less punishment than they expected or none at all

**d** My sister and I **fell out** when she discovered that I had read her diaries.
  *i* stop being friends, quarrel
  *ii* drop out of something

**e** I **get on with** my brothers and sisters. We rarely argue.
  *i* have a friendly relationship with
  *ii* make progress with

**2** Form negatives by adding *mis-* (badly or wrongly) or *dis-* (opposite of).

behave    lead      own       judge
honour    manage    please    obey

## GETTING STREETWISE! 😦
### Expressing opinions

**1** Write down as many different ways of expressing your opinion as you can.

**2** You are going to hear what David's father thinks about the problem and what the solutions are. Try and predict what he is going to say before you listen.

**3** Answer these questions.

**a** In what way does he treat David differently from his mother?

**b** In what ways were his opinions the same or different from what you expected?

**4** What expressions did David's father use to express his opinions. How many of these were you able to list in task 1?

## TALKING POINT
Work in a group of three.
Two of you should take turns to share your opinions on how you would deal with a difficult child like David.

The third member should listen, and write down the expressions you used to exchange opinions. At the end the observer should lead a discussion on these questions.

**a** What expressions did you use to express your own opinions?

**b** Did you try and find out what your partner thought or not? Why? How?

# BETWEEN THE LINES

## *WARM-UP*

Here is an example of a very, very short story by an American writer called Richard Brautigan. Read it carefully and then discuss the questions with a partner.

'It's hard to live in a studio apartment in San Jose with a man who's learning to play the violin.' That's what she told the police when she handed them the empty revolver.

a   What *facts* does the story give you?
b   What do you think has happened?
c   Why did it happen?
d   What are the possible relationships between the violin player and the woman?
e   How would you describe the woman's mood?
f   What other information would you like?

Join with another pair and share your conclusions. In what ways are they similar? Be prepared to report these back to the class.

## *Improve your writing*

### Telling a story

1   Setting
    Decide how you will locate your story in time and place.
    *Once there lived a rich man with two wives...*
    *Katya switched off the lights; the window went dark, it was very early...*

2   Viewpoint
    Now decide who is telling the story. If you are telling the story personally, use the first person (I); if not, use the third person (e.g. a man/woman, she/he, etc.)

3   Plot: Sequence
    Decide in which order or sequence you will place the events in your story. It is common to tell a story in the order in which it happens, but newspapers often change the order and begin with the most dramatic part of the story.

4   Plot: Tense
    When you tell a story you usually use past tenses. Progressive forms are useful for describing what is happening in the background. Linking words like *while* make it clear that events are happening at the same time. The simple past tense tells the story. You can tell the story in the present to make the events more dramatic, but do *not* mix past and present tenses.

5   Audience
    Always think about who will be reading or listening to your story. What do they know already? What do they need to know? What style of language is it appropriate to use? Should it be formal or informal?

## *PRACTICE 1*

1   Insert words from the box into these opening sentences to short stories.

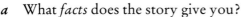

opened   looked   screams   rained
seeing   didn't leave   went

a   Marta was nineteen. She _____ (1) out over the roof of the skyscraper, and _____ (2) the city below, she was overcome with dizziness.
b   Mr Frensham _____ (3) his shop at eight-thirty, but it was past nine when the woman and the child _____ (4) in.
c   I come into the kitchen quietly. My mother _____ (5). 'What are you doing here?'
d   It _____ (6) all week long and Mrs Martins _____ (7) the house even to go shopping.

2   Put the verbs in brackets into an appropriate form.
    It was nightfall. Arthur _____ (walk) slowly though the city streets. He _____ (think) about Marcia. Why _____ she _____ him? (leave) He _____ (can) offer no explanation. All around him people _____ (rush) home to their families.

## Improve your wordpower

### Adverbs

These are very useful in story-telling. They add interest by telling us how someone did something. Many adverbs are formed by adding -*ly* to the adjective, but there are spelling changes.

1   Complete this table before outlining the rules for spelling changes.

| adjective | adverb |
| --- | --- |
| nervous | —— |
| —— | happily |
| busy | |
| —— | comfortably |
| miserable | —— |
| —— | systematically |
| basic | —— |

Note the exception: public/publicly

2   When you do *Practice 2*, use as many of these, and other adjectives/adverbs as you can.

## PRACTICE 2

Work in groups of three.

1   Arrange the pictures in order to tell a story.
2   Decide on something dramatic which happens after the last frame.
3   Write a group version of your story. Start with the most dramatic part before describing the events leading up to it. Invent

any details that you want to make the story more interesting. Be ready to read your story to the class.

## LISTENING

### His heavy metal's driving me mad

Most of us tell stories. Here is Kate's. Listen to her story and find out what her problem is.

Work in a small group.

*a*   Imagine that Ian decides to tell Kate why he has changed his behaviour. Write the conversation. To do this you must decide on the reason for his change. Here are some possibilities.

- Ian is bored with his current life.
- He has started to experiment with drugs.
- He did this because he had met some new friends.
- He has found something that he really likes.

Can you think of any others?

*b*   What do you think will happen?

### Use and usage

### Adjective + preposition

After some adjectives we can use a preposition (e.g. *of*, *about*).

Here are some common 'adjective + preposition' combinations which are to do with feelings towards people.

afraid of, angry with, annoyed with, fed up with, ashamed of, bored with, disappointed with/in, interested in, keen on, fond of, frustrated with, pleased with, tired of, worried about.

1   Sort the adjectives out into those which describe positive feelings and those which describe negative ones.
2   Which ones could you use to describe Kate's relationship with Ian?

Example
*She is worried about him.*

## WRITING

Write Kate and Ian's story. Consider each of the points in the *Improve your writing* guidelines before you start.

# HERE IS THE NEWS

## READING
Read the text and answer the questions.

### NEWS OR ENTERTAINMENT?
Where does your knowledge of the news come from? In Britain, 62% of the population gets its information from television, 23% from newspapers and 13% from radio. A TV news broadcast is therefore an important source of information. However, are TV news broadcasts more concerned with entertainment than information? Look at the facts:

News broadcasts are introduced by the same kind of lively music as other programmes on TV. Programmes also begin with headlines designed to attract the viewer.

The news-readers are often attractive and friendly. They sit behind impressive desks and often feature in newspaper articles about their private lives.

The news items may be serious but they are often followed by advertisements which make them less significant.

The average length of items is only forty-five seconds. This means even important items may only get three or four minutes of coverage. As a result TV news cannot deal with complex issues and when it does it tends to simplify them.

Issues are also trivialized by the proportion of *soft* items in each broadcast. These are often placed at the end of the news and concern the Royal Family, animals, 'strange but true' items, etc.

1  In what ways is the television news like any other form of entertainment on TV?
2  What is the writer concerned about in television news?

## LISTENING  ☹
Listen to the start of this television news broadcast. There are five headlines to attract the viewer. What topics do they cover?

### Glossary
**issues:** important subjects that people discuss, and argue about

**trivialized:** made to seem unimportant

## TALKING POINT
Answer these questions.

*a*  Do you agree that television trivializes the news? Why/Why not?

*b*  Which of these provides the best and most reliable source of news in your country: newspapers, television or radio?

*c*  Here are ten stories for a TV news programme. Choose six and decide on the order in which they will appear.

1  Flood in Germany
2  Local fishing boat hit by mystery submarine
3  Panda in Mexican zoo has baby
4  Unemployment rises again
5  Royal visit to new hospital
6  International rescue of whale trapped in Arctic ice
7  Top politician murdered
8  Sports results
9  Storm in India kills 400 people
10  Film star's child is kidnapped

*d*  Decide on three main headlines which are most likely to attract viewers.

### Research
*Aims:*
1)  to analyse major news broadcasts for one evening in terms of:
**a**  the style of presentation
**b**  the news items they cover
**c**  the proportions of 'soft' and 'hard' news.
2)  to compare your results and conclusions in a class discussion.

### Hot tips!

- In groups or as a class, decide on the evening on which you will try to watch the news broadcasts.
- If possible, try to watch different broadcasts and compare them.
- Agree on the points of comparison before you watch the broadcasts.
- If you are working with a partner, divide the task up and investigate different areas.

# STREETWISE
## ISSUE 4

## FAITH IN THE FUTURE?

Serious build-ups of toxic wastes

Small community sharing communal facilities

## THE INEVITABLE GAP?

## THE BIG DAY

# FAITH IN THE FUTURE?

## WARM-UP

List the main problems affecting the world today. Do you think the problems we will face in the future will be the same or different?

## READING

Read the text and answer the questions.

### PUTTING FAITH IN THE FUTURE

Faith Popcorn is America's most prominent futurologist. She predicts how tastes will change and the nation's biggest companies pay big money for this. She has seen the future and believes that there are two options.

In one of the options, the streets ten years from now are ruled by an uneducated underclass, and armed guards pick up children from school and return them to their walled communities. Atmospheric pollution is so awful that you can drive your car only three times a week, and the build-up of toxic waste is so bad that every year another medium-sized city has to be evacuated.

In the other, by the year 2010 we live in small communities of 50 families, sharing goods and services and communal facilities such as kitchens, day-care centres and clinics. Mega-companies have given way to smaller, socially responsible businesses and most people work at home, electronically wired to the larger world. We use resources carefully, replacing what we consume, healing the planet.

The choice is ours. Popcorn is essentially optimistic about how things will turn out because all it takes is positive action. 'It is a source of strength to change the future,' she says in her book, *The Popcorn Report*.

So what is going to happen in the first part of the twenty-first century?

People will turn to home and self-protection. We will be more responsive to the needs of older people and anti-ageing drugs may extend life by twenty years. There will be foods to reduce stress, increase energy or help us to sleep, according to individual needs. People will continue to see the home as somewhere to escape from a difficult world, and shopping as we know it will have disappeared by 2015. It will all be done electronically. The things we buy will be selected on screen and delivered to our door.

By the end of the twenty-first century, computers will be taking people on trips to the Himalayas or the Amazon, or back to the French revolution. We'll be exercising our thinking in brain gyms and there will also be armies of androids walking dogs and driving buses.

'We are an endangered species,' says Faith Popcorn, 'facing environmental, economic, educational, and political crises. We don't look to the future as the place we want to live in any more.'

But she predicts the world will be saved. First by the recognition of how bad things have become, then by anger and finally, by the power of positive action.

'After anger comes the strength that will give us the chance to shape up the future. We can only stand pessimism for so long.'

1 What do we know about Faith Popcorn from this article?
2 Why is she 'essentially optimistic' about the future?
3 Do you think her predictions will come true? Why/Why not?

## VOCABULARY

Find words or phrases in the text that mean:

a possibilities, choices
b increase of poisonous rubbish
c shared and for the use of all
d very large companies
e hopeful, believes that things will happen in the best possible way
f will be chosen
g robots with human characteristics
h class of animals that is in danger of dying out
i negative feelings that the worst will happen

## PRONUNCIATION 😐

### Word stress – suffixes

1 Mark the main stress on these words.

| | |
|---|---|
| electronic | electronically |
| environmental | environmentally |
| educational | educationally |
| political | politically |

2 Listen and check your answers. Are the suffixes stressed or not?
3 Listen and repeat. Take care with the sound /ə/.

*Glossary*

**underclass:** group of people at a lower level than normal society in terms of money, jobs, housing, etc.

**crises:** times of great difficulty and danger (*singular* crisis)

### Future forms

1 Look through the article to find as many different ways of expressing the future as you can.

2 Which of these do you use for an event:

  *a* that will be in progress at a certain time in the future.
  *b* which will be over not later than a certain time?
  *c* when the person doing the thing is not known or not important?

3 Complete the passage with *will* or *going to*.

  *Will* and *going to* are both used for predictions. However, we use ____ for a prediction based on the present situation (e.g. what we can see is going to happen). *Look, the plane is on fire! It's* ____ *crash.* We use ____ for a prediction (what we think will happen). *One day people* ____ *live in space.*

## PRACTICE

1 Choose the best form. Give reasons for your answers.

  *a* What is that crystal ball for? I think *he'll/he's going to* look into the future.
  *b* He's got a new job. *He's going to do/He'll do* research into the future.
  *c* I think that people *will/are going to* travel to Mars one of these days.
  *d* The building will take ten years. If they start today they *won't have finished/will be finishing* by the year 2000.

2 Expand these using the future perfect.

  Example
  By/2015 shopping disappear.
  *By the year 2015 shopping will have disappeared.*

  *a* By/end/twenty-first century doctors perfect anti-ageing drugs.
  *b* By/end/next century robots be replaced.
  *c* If we are not careful we destroy/world's resources in five years' time.
  *d* By/2010 I use computers/twenty years.

3 Rewrite these sentences to keep the same meaning. Start with the words provided.

  *a* Someone will perfect anti-ageing drugs.
  Anti-ageing drugs ____ .
  *b* We will encourage children to study more.
  Children will ____ .
  *c* More people will work at home.
  More work ____ .
  *d* People will use more and more computers.
  More ____ .

### I hope so and I hope not

'Do you think things will improve in the future?' 'I hope so.' (= I hope things will improve.)

'Will pollution get worse?' 'I hope not.' (= I hope pollution won't get worse.)

Answer the questions with *I hope so* or *I hope not*.

  *a* Has someone stolen your bike?
  *b* Have you passed your exams?
  *c* Is there any homework to do?

## LISTENING

Faith Popcorn predicts that computers will soon be taking people on mind trips to the Himalayas or the Amazon. The technology is called Virtual Reality.

1 Discuss these questions before listening to Andrea Lynch's report.

  Why are scientists interested in developing machines that can take you on mind trips? Where would *you* like to go on a mind trip?

2 Listen again and decide if these statements are true or false according to the tape.

  *a* There are no limits to Virtual Reality.
  *b* Virtual Reality is created by being in a special room.
  *c* Virtual Reality is not yet available for use.
  *d* It's only use will be commercial.
  *e* Virtual Reality is an important invention.
  *f* Virtual Reality might be misused.

3 What are some of the things Virtual Reality can do?

4 Do you think Virtual Reality is a good idea or not? Why? Which uses of Virtual Reality would appeal to you most?

## WRITING

A lifestyle magazine has asked its younger readers for entries to a competition entitled *Life in the year 2010*. Use the material in this issue to predict what life will be like in your country. Will it be safe to go out? Will more people work from home? How will family life change?

Start your paragraph:

*I have seen the future. By the year 2010 . . .*

# THE BIG DAY

## READING

Complete each blank in the text with a word from the box below.

> casual  chew  have  untidy  looks
> nervousness  take  check  mended
> wearing  bag  wear

### THE SMART WAY TO GET ON

Doing well in an interview may be an important part of getting a university place, a job, or a pass in an important exam. However, many young people fail to create that vital first impression because their appearance lets them down. *Streetwise* looks at how to dress and behave on the big day.

Don't fiddle with your hair, or _____ your nails or fingers. It can be very off-putting, and only highlights your _____ .

Don't wear clothes that are scruffy and _____ .

Don't _____ along your personal stereo – switched on or off!

Don't take a plastic _____ – even for important documents like your CV or exam card – it always _____ like you're carrying your dirty washing.

Don't wear _____ shoes – sneakers are out!

Do enter the interview room _____ a bright and friendly smile, it counts for a lot ...

Do dress smartly. Whether your clothes are old or new, _____ them washed and pressed – dry-cleaned if necessary.

Do _____ your shoes in advance. Have them _____ if necessary.

Do _____ a shirt and tie if the interview demands it.

### Glossary

**fiddle:** keep moving or touching something

**scruffy:** dirty (and untidy) in appearance

**CV:** abbreviation for curriculum vitae – a brief written account of the main events of your life, details about yourself, your education, hobbies, jobs, etc.

## LISTENING 😐

### Surviving an interview

Patrick Chan is having his first interview next week. Stephen Frazer took Patrick to see Sarah Brown, an expert on interview techniques. Listen and answer the questions below.

1  Decide if these statements are true or false according to the tape.

*a*  Pat is planning to wear his jacket.

*b*  His interview starts at eleven.

*c*  He is going by car.

*d*  Pat should try and talk to the other interviewees.

*e*  Pat should sit down as soon as he goes in the interview room.

*f*  He should always shake hands with the interviewers.

*g*  He should always look at the interviewers while he is talking.

*h*  He should ask questions.

2  In your opinion, what are the three most important pieces of advice?

## Grammar quiz

### Future forms

1  Look at these examples. What do the verbs in italics have in common?

*a*  The interview *starts* at eleven.

*b*  I hope you *do* well.

*c*  When they *are* ready for you, someone will come and get you.

*d*  Dad *is driving* me.

2  Match the examples above to these uses.

*i*  for future events resulting from a present plan, programme or arrangement

*ii*  for the future after time expressions like *as soon as, before, after*, etc.

*iii*  for future reference in clauses after *I hope, I assume*, etc.

*iv*  for future events which are seen as certain, either because they are fixed by calendar or timetable, or because they are part of an unalterable plan

## PRACTICE 1

1 Pat is talking to a friend about his interview. Fill in the blanks. You may need more than one word in each space.

John: Hi Pat, when _____ (1) interview?
Pat: Next Friday.
John: _____ (2)?
Pat: It starts at eleven.
John: How _____ (3)?
Pat: My dad's driving me.
John: I _____ (4) next week.
Pat: Really! What is the interview for?
John: A scholarship to visit Japan.
Pat: What will you do when you get there?
John: Not much. It's really just a chance to see the country and learn some Japanese.
Pat: Well, I hope _____ (5). Let me know how you get on.
John: I'll get in touch as soon as _____ (6) the result of the interview.

2 What would you say in each of these situations? Use an appropriate future form.

a You need to tell a friend the time of next week's English exam.
b You need to tell a young child tomorrow's day and date.
c A friend has invited you for dinner. Tell him about your travel plans for getting to his house.
d Imagine that you have booked a guided tour for a group of foreign students. Tell them about their programme.

### Improve your wordpower

1 Match these verbs to the definitions.
put someone off    get worked up
turn someone down

a refuse or reject someone
b discourage
c become angry or excited

2 Complete these sentences with a suitable form of the verbs in exercise 1.

a I went for the interview but they _____ because I had no experience.
b Nothing _____ her _____ once she had made up her mind.
c He _____ about the article because he did not agree with the writer's views.

## GETTING STREETWISE! 

### Fear and anxiety

1 Which of these adjectives best describes the way you normally feel before an important exam?

a flustered = nervous and confused
b cool, calm and collected = unemotional and unexcited
c anxious = nervous and worried
d confident = unworried, sure that you will do well
e sick = ill in your stomach

Now listen to what the *Streetwise* panel feel about taking exams and complete the table.

| | Worries about |
|---|---|
| **Mike** | |
| **Alex** | |
| **Sandra** | |
| **Alan** | |

2 Listen again and see which of these expressions for expressing fear and anxiety were used by the panel.
*What if . . .*
*I'm absolutely dreading it . . .*
*I'm terrified by . . .*
*The thought of . . . makes me sick*
*I just don't think I can . . .*
*I'm afraid of . . .*

3 Which panel members do you identify with? Why?

## PRACTICE 2

Work with a partner.

I'm not looking forward to the party. What if I don't know anybody?

Student A
You are going to do something you are not looking forward to (e.g. go to a party). Tell your partner about your anxieties.

Student B
Listen to the problem but try your best to reassure your partner.
These expressions may help:

*Don't worry. It'll be alright.*
*I'll be thinking of you.*
*I'm sure everything will go well.*
*I'll keep my fingers crossed (for you).*

# THE INEVITABLE GAP?

3 Write your own scene about a typical parent/child conflict in your country. Perform your scene and vote for the best one.

## *READING*

Read these extracts before discussing the questions in small groups.

### HOW NOT TO TALK TO YOUR MOTHER

*You are about to leave the house:*

'Where are you going?'

'Out.'

'Out where?'

'Just out.'

'Who are you going with?'

'A friend.'

'Which friend?'

'Mom, just a friend, okay? Do you have to know everything?'

'I don't have to know everything. I just want to know who you're going out with.'

'Debby, okay?'

'Do I know Debby?'

'She's just a friend, okay?'

'Well, where are you going?'

'Out!'

*You have just come home:*

'Hi, Mom, did anyone call?'

'You did get one call, but I forgot to ask who it was.'

'Male or female?'

'Male.'

'And you didn't ask! Thanks Mom, thanks a lot, I really appreciate it. For all I know it was the most important phone call of my life!'

*You have just hung up the telephone:*

'Who was that, dear?'

'Can't a person have some privacy once in a while!'

*You have just returned from school:*

'How did you do on the science test?'

'Can't you ever stop asking me questions!'

'I really think that's uncalled for. If I ask, you tell me I'm prying. If I don't ask, you say I'm not interested. I can't win.'

'That's right, Mom, you can't.'

1 Do you recognise any of these situations? Would these conversations occur in your country? Why/Why not?

2 Work with a partner and role-play any two of these situations. Try your best to use the right tone and intonation.

### *TALKING POINT*

I hate it when my dad says 'Don't argue! Don't answer back!'

I know they like to be independent but they can be so rude.

Work in small groups. Make sure that you note down the answers to all these questions. You will need these for the *Writing* exercise.

*a* Do you think that friction between young people and their parents is inevitable? Why?

*b* What are the reasons for conflict and friction? What subjects and topics do you agree on? What subjects and topics do you usually disagree on? What are the areas that cause most problems?

*c* What will you do to cut down on friction when you are parents yourselves?

### *Improve your wordpower*

In Britain, the use of the telephone can be a major source of friction between parents and young people. Here are some common expressions used in connection with the telephone. Explain the meaning of each one.

*a* Speaking.

*b* Please hang on.

*c* Why don't you give me a ring?

*d* Is Maria in, please?

*e* Who's calling?

1 Listen and follow the instructions on the tape. Use an appropriate expression each time you hear the beep.

2 Prepare and act out your own telephone conversation using some of the expressions above.

**Glossary**

**Mom:** Mother; spelt Mum in British English

**uncalled for:** unfair and unjustified

**prying:** trying to find out about someone's private affairs

## *Improve your writing*

### Discussion

A discussion essay puts forward two or more views on a subject, for example, the case *for* and *against* something, or outlining the *advantages* and *disadvantages* of doing something. Your own opinion usually comes at the end.

### Stage 1

Map out the content. One way you can do this is to divide a sheet of paper into two. Note the main points *for* in the left-hand column; the points *against* in the right. If you leave space after each point you can add ideas from your own experience, etc.

### Stage 2

Turn your list of points into a first draft. In Paragraph 1 you need to give an idea of what your essay is about.

Then introduce the points from your left-hand column. If the points are short you can group two or three in one paragraph. If not, use a new paragraph for each new main point. Signal each separate point clearly by using expressions like:

*The first reason why . . .*
*The second argument for thinking . . .*
*In addition, . . ./Furthermore, . . .*

In the next section, give points from the right-hand column. Make the contrast between sections clear, with expressions like:

*In contrast, . . ./However, . . ./On the other hand, . . .*

You should also continue to signal separate points clearly.

In the final paragraph you should summarize and give your own view with reasons. This is marked by expressions like:

*To sum up, . . ./In conclusion . . .*
*On balance, . . ./On the whole, . . .*

### Stage 3

Check your work. Is the spelling, punctuation, and grammar correct? Are the arguments clear and logical? Write your essay out neatly.

## PRACTICE

1 These are notes for a composition entitled *Young people today don't care. Discuss.* Put the notes into two columns. One *for* and the other *against.*

Young people today don't care about anything or anyone.
They take part in charity events.
They don't seem to want to do anything for themselves.
Very few young people are vandals.
The only thing young people worry about is fashion and the way they look.
In lots of places there are no facilities for the young.
Young people sit around moaning.
People who complain about the young often have no contact with them.
Young people would do more if they were allowed to.
The young vandalize property when they are bored.

Can you add any more points to either list?

2 Look at your two lists and decide on the order in which the points might appear if you were writing an essay. Use your points and these expressions to help you to write the main paragraphs of the essay.

*Introduction*
Many older people argue that . . .

*Paragraph One* (The arguments for)

The main reason is that they think . . .
Another reason is that they believe . . .
Furthermore they argue . . .

*Paragraph Two* (The arguments against)

However, . . .
The evidence is . . .
What is more, young people . . .

*Conclusion*
To sum up, . . .

## WRITING

Use the notes you have gathered to help you to write a discussion essay entitled:

*Children should always obey their parents*

Put the case *for* and *against*, using examples from your own experience.
In the concluding paragraph you should outline your own opinion.

# RHYTHM AND STRESS

rhythm
poem
unique
unless
piano
reveal
proverb
contain
another

## QUIZ 😦

### Syllables and stress

A syllable is a word or part of a word that usually contains a vowel sound. Each of these words has two syllables. Mark the syllable which is normally stressed.

*a* English  *d* fourteen  *g* sixteen
*b* today    *e* forty     *h* written
*c* table    *f* sixty     *i* retain

1 Work in pairs and discuss what happens if you stress the other part of the word?
2 Now listen to a comment on the task you have just done.

## READING/LISTENING 😦

### STRESS-TIMING

1 Look at these sentences. The stressed syllables are underlined.
*a* I had a steak for lunch.
*b* I had a hamburger for lunch.
   Which sentence takes longest to read?

2 Now listen to how the sentences are read before studying the text below.

The world's languages can generally be divided into two categories. They are either 'stress-timed' or 'syllable-timed'.

Many European languages are syllable-timed. In these, speakers say all the syllables at an approximately uniform rate. The more syllables there are in a phrase the longer it takes to say.

English is a stress-timed language. When we speak English, all the stressed syllables in our sentences tend to come at roughly identical intervals of time. If there are a few syllables between the stresses, they are said more slowly. If a larger number of syllables comes between two stresses, they are said more quickly. Thus the sentences we looked at would, if spoken by the same speaker, take the same number of seconds to say, even though they contain different numbers of words or syllables, because they both contain three stressed syllables. The vowels in unstressed syllables often become neutral or weak vowels represented by the symbol /ə/.

### Glossary

**in gibbers:** in a fast and confused manner

3 Is your first language stress-timed or syllable-timed? If you are not sure, try counting.
4 Practise these examples before listening to how they can be read.
*a* I ate a nice big steak.
*b* I ate a lovely tender chicken.
*c* I ate a delicious mouth-watering pineapple.

## RHYTHM

The alternation of stressed and unstressed syllables, with the stressed syllables occurring on a regular beat, produces the characteristic rhythm of English. This is most apparent in poetry and verse.

Listen to an example before answering the questions.

1 What effect is the poet trying to achieve? Do you think he succeeds? Why/Why not?
2 Now look at this example of a limerick.

Every night father fills me with dread
When he sits at the foot of my bed
I'd not mind that he speaks
In gibbers and squeaks
But for seventeen years he's been dead!

*Roger McGough*

*a* How many lines are there?
*b* Which lines rhyme? (i.e. end with a very similar sound)
*c* Three lines share the same rhyme. Label these *a*. Label the remaining lines *b*.
*d* Count the stressed syllables in the *a* lines and the *b* lines. Listen to the tape.
3 Look at this example of a limerick by the same poet, and put in the missing words.

*on top of   Thursday   feet   young   bed head*

There was a _____ man name of Fred,
Who spent every _____ in _____ ;
He lay with his _____
Outside of the sheet,
And the pillows _____ his _____ .

Now listen to a recording of the limerick.

### Research

*Aim:*
1) to learn and recite an English limerick or poem. If you want to, try writing your own.

# GRAMMAR REVIEW ISSUES 3 AND 4

## PAST TENSES

The options for talking about the past in English include the past simple, past progressive, *used to/would*, the past perfect, past perfect progressive, and present perfect.

| Uses | Examples |
|---|---|
| 1 Past simple: for a number of events which took place one after the other in the past. | *He came in, went to the window and opened it.* |
| 2 Past progressive: for an event which was in progress when another event happened. | *She was sleeping when the accident happened.* |
| 3 Past progressive: to set the scene and provide the background for a story. | *The sun was shining brightly when Bob woke up.* |
| 4 Past perfect: for an event which happened before another in the past. | *I went home because I had left my homework at home.* |
| 5 Past perfect progressive: to talk about an event that was in progress up to the past time we are thinking about. | *I was very tired. I had been playing basketball all afternoon.* |
| 6 Past perfect progressive: to show that an action was frequently repeated, before a past time we are thinking about. | *She had been biting her nails for years, but last month she gave up.* |
| 7 Present perfect: for actions in the past that are not given a specific time. | *My brother has visited Australia.* |

## FUTURE IN THE PAST

The future in the past can be expressed by *was going to*, *was about to*, and *was on the point of*.

| Uses | Examples |
|---|---|
| 1 To refer to events which were planned to take place and which did take place. | *I was about to go to bed when I noticed a funny smell.* *When I got there she was about to leave, so I didn't really speak to her.* |
| 2 To refer to events which were intended but which did not happen at the time because something interrupted or prevented them. | *I was about to go on holiday, but the airline went on strike.* *I was going to give her the money, but she didn't come.* |

### Notes

*Was about to* and *was on the point of* both carry the suggestion that the 'future in the past' event is very near.

*It was 8.59 and the lesson was on the point of starting when he walked in.*

When we use *I was going to see him* or *I was about to see him* we need further information to know whether the meeting took place or was prevented from taking place.

## FUTURE FORMS

| Uses | Examples |
|---|---|
| 1 *be going to*: for an intention. | *I'm going to do my homework this evening.* |
| 2 *be going to*: to indicate that something is probable. | *I think the plane is going to crash.* |
| 3 *will/shall*: to make predictions. | *We will all live in cities in future.* *I think the sun will shine tomorrow.* |
| 4 Future progressive: for an event that will be in progress at a certain time in the future. | *I'll be doing my exam this time next week.* |
| 5 Future perfect: for an event which will be over not later than a certain time. | *Will you have finished by midnight?* *He will have gone home by then.* |
| 6 Future passive: for the future where the person or agent doing the thing is not known or not important. | *It will be done.* |

## Notes

*Will* (not *going to*) is used to express a sudden decision to do something in the future.

*'Oh, the phone is ringing.' 'I'll answer it.'*
*I'm bored. What can I do? I know! I'll clean my bike.*

*Shall* is most commonly used:

*a*   to offer to do something.
   *Shall I help you carry the shopping?*
*b*   in suggestions.
   *Shall we go and see a film tonight?*
*c*   in requests for instructions.
   *What shall I do next?*

## FUTURE FORMS – PRESENT TENSES

| Uses | Examples |
|---|---|
| 1   Present progressive: for future events resulting from a present plan, programme or arrangement. | *I'm planning to wear a jacket.*<br>*Dad's driving me.*<br>*I'm thinking of studying medicine.* |
| 2   Simple present: for the future in certain types of subordinate clause, especially adverbial time clauses and conditional clauses. Conjunctions which go with the present tense in this way are *after*, *before*, *once*, *until*, *when*, *as soon as*, *if*, *even if*, *unless*, *as long as*. | *When they are ready for you, someone will come and get you.*<br>*As soon as he arrives, we'll start the lesson.*<br>*She'll wait until you phone her.* |
| 3   Simple present: 'that' clauses following *hope*, *assume*, *suppose*, etc. can also contain a verb in the present tense referring to the future. | *I hope you do well.*<br>*Let's assume the team gets to the final. Where...* |
| 4   Simple present: for future events which are seen as absolutely certain, either because they are determined in advance by calendar or timetable, or because they are part of an unalterable plan. | *Tomorrow is a Saturday.*<br>*The interview starts at eleven.*<br>*He retires next month.* |

# GRAMMAR PRACTICE

## A

1   Complete the sentences with an appropriate form of the verb (past simple, past progressive or past perfect).

Example
He *wasn't playing* (not play) there. He *had left* (leave) before I *arrived* (arrive).

*a*   The concert _____ (begin) at nine last night.
*b*   She _____ (write) a letter when somebody _____ (come) in.
*c*   He _____ (do) five grammar exercises by lunch-time.
*d*   I _____ (see) him a month ago. He _____ (not go) to America yet.
*e*   He said that he _____ (not see) her for years.
*f*   It _____ (rain) at the time of the accident.

2   Choose the correct future form.

Example
I don't feel very well. I'm *going to be*/I'll be sick.

*a*   'How do you use this' 'That's easy, I'll show/I'm going to show you.'
*b*   The train will have left/will be leaving by nine o'clock.
*c*   If he will go/goes, I'll stay.
*d*   This time next week we will sit/ will be sitting on the beach.
*e*   The radios will be made/will make in Japan.
*f*   'What are you doing tonight?' 'I'm going to/I'll repair my bike.'

3   Join an idea in A with an idea from B. Make sentences using *was/were going to* and the verb in brackets.

| A | B |
|---|---|
| *a*   He (study) medicine at university | but it was closed. |
| *b*   I (return) the book I borrowed | but we had pasta in the end. |
| *c*   I (go) to the concert | but he broke his hand. |
| *d*   We (fly) there | but they bought a computer instead. |
| *e*   He (play) in goal | but I couldn't get tickets. |
| *f*   They (buy) a typewriter | but he failed his exams. |
| *g*   We (have) pizza for lunch | but the airline went on strike. |
| *h*   They (visit) the museum | until she found out he was already married. |
| *i*   She (marry) him | but I left it at home. |

## B

**1** Finish each of the sentences so that it means exactly the same as the sentence printed before it. Use verbs that express the idea of something happening in the future.

Example
I've decided to fly to Manchester next week.
*I'm flying to Manchester next week.*

**a** I've decided to go to Italy for my holidays.
I'm _____ .

**b** We will go on a city tour on arrival.
As soon as _____ .

**c** The time of the next bus to London is 22.15.
The London bus _____ .

**d** I've decided to start learning Spanish next month.
I'm _____ .

**e** I predict a rise in prices next year.
In my opinion, _____ .

**f** Someone will finish it.
It _____ .

**2** Use *was going to* or *was about to* to write sentences for each situation.

Example
**a** *They were going to drive away when they discovered that their wheels were missing.*

**3** Jane and Jim are talking about their weekend plans. Complete the conversation.

*Jane:* Hi Jim! What ____ (*a*)?
*Jim:* I'm going to see my grandmother on Sunday Why?
*Jane:* There ____ (*b*) a concert at the Apollo on Saturday.
*Jim:* Who ____ (*c*)?
*Jane:* Bruce Springsteen.
*Jim:* Have ____ (*d*)?
*Jane:* Yes, and I've got an extra ticket for you!
*Jim:* That's fantastic. What time ____ (*e*)?
*Jane:* At eight. Let's meet my house at seven.
*Jim:* Great! I ____ (*f*) then.
*Jane:* I ____ (*g*) forward to seeing you.

**4** Make the necessary changes and additions to write complete sentences.

Dear Carmen
**a** I hope/be well. I be fine.
**b** This time next week, I do/exams.
**c** I study very hard for/last month.
**d** As soon as/exams finish we go/holiday.
**e** I really need/holiday by the time/exams be over!
**f** This year we go/the north of Spain.
**g** I look foward/it very, very much.
**h** I write/you again when/get there.
Yours,
Jim
**i** PS I be about to put this/the post when/get your good luck card.
**j** It be lovely! Thanks for thinking/me.

## C

**1** Read this joke.
A naughty child was annoying all the passengers on the flight from London to New York. At last, one man couldn't stand it any more. 'Hey, kid,' he shouted, 'Why don't you go outside and play?'
Write your own joke in English.

**2** Imagine that you are working in a travel agency. You have planned a week's dream holiday for a visitor from outer space. Use appropriate future tenses to tell your client about the holiday.

Example
*On Monday you leave for the Caribbean. As soon as you arrive, you will be taken to a luxury hotel...*

# *Wise up!*

# GRAMMAR

## KNOWING GRAMMAR

1 Which of these statements do you agree with? Why?
- We cannot get the grammar of a language right unless we are able to state the rule.
- Knowledge of grammatical rules does not necessarily mean that we speak accurately.
- Accuracy can only come as a result of practice.
- It is useful to learn grammatical rules because they can help us when we check what we say or write.

2 In pairs, see if you can agree on what it means to 'know your grammar'.

## IMPROVING YOUR GRAMMAR

Here are some ideas for improving your grammar.
- Use a reference grammar and/or a grammar practice book to work on areas where you make mistakes.
- Keep a grammar notebook that gives you key information about your own problem areas. Always include examples as well as explanations.
- Create your own practice materials. For example, create your own blanks in a text by removing 'grammar' words such as articles, verbs and pronouns. Leave the text before trying to complete it. Note the items you got wrong and look them up in a grammar book, or ask your teacher.

1 Create a practice exercise and use it.

## WHAT THE EXAMINER WANTS

Here are some of the techniques examiners use to test your knowledge of grammar.
- Gap filling
- Transformations
- Multiple choice
- Sentence or dialogue completion

1 List the question types used to test grammar in any exam you may be preparing for.

## USING CONTEXT

### Multiple choice and filling in the blanks

The grammatical form we choose depends on context and meaning, so:
- read the whole sentence or text before you begin, so that you have an idea of the meaning.

- look at the words before and after a blank to see what help they give you. For example:
  *He has lived there since the house ___ built.*
  *Built* (past participle) suggests a part of the verb is missing. *House* indicates that it will be singular.
  Don't forget to look for words or phrases which provide clues to tense, such as *yesterday*, *next week*.
- note the parts of speech when you learn new words (e.g. *post* can be a verb and a noun).
- say the complete sentence (aloud or silently to yourself) to see if it sounds right to you.

### Transformations

Read each sentence carefully to assess the kind of transformation that is required. Typical changes include:
- Changes of word order and verb form.
  *He got lost because he didn't have a map.*
  *If he had had a map he wouldn't have got lost.*
- Changes from active to passive or vice versa.
  *They are building a new house on the island.*
  *A new house is being built on the island.*
- Changes from direct to indirect speech or vice versa.
  *'I saw him,' she said to Tom.*
  *She told Tom that she had seen him.*
- Changes of expression to keep the same meaning.
  *I will never forget him.*
  *I will always remember him.*

### Sentence or dialogue completion

As always, read the whole sentence/dialogue before you begin, and remember that if the completion exercise is a text or a dialogue it can be the sentence after the gap that provides the vital clue as much as the sentence before it.

Matt  **What would you like to drink?**
Sue  *I'd like coffee, please.*

1 What type of word should go in these gaps? Circle the clue that helps you find the answer.

a  I tried to ___ where I had seen him before.
b  Give me an ice-cream and ___ coke, please.
c  He was old and ___ .
d  I will never ___ him.
e  We ___ going to the cinema tomorrow.
f  We ___ going to the cinema because our father always buys us ice-cream.
g  The bird flew home ___ its nest.
h  She was a teacher when we met, but she ___ in a museum before training as a teacher.
i  ___ looked everywhere but I couldn't find ___ .
j  ___ do you want to do when you grow up?

# STREETWISE
## ISSUE 5

## VISITORS FROM SPACE

Ancient markings on the plain of Nazca in Peru

Markings in a field in England, 1990

## WHAT IS YOUR REACTION TIME?

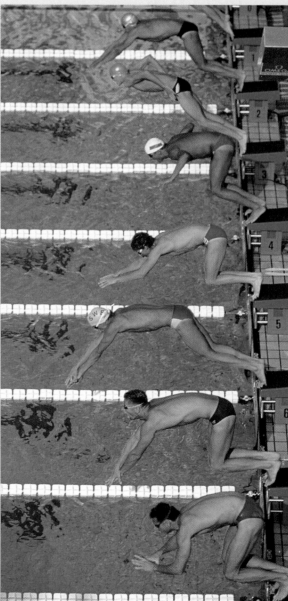

## RIGHT TO BE LEFT

Anaxagoras asserts that it is his possession of hands that makes human beings the most intelligent of animals; but surely the reasonable point of view is that it is because they are the most intelligent animal that they have got hands.

*Aristotle*

# VISITORS FROM SPACE

## WARM-UP

A UFO is an Unidentified Flying Object. It is a technical term for an object seen in the sky or landing on earth which cannot be identified. It could be anything from an air-craft to a flying paper bag. It is, however, often used to mean flying saucers or spaceships from outer space.

Work individually and draw a diagram of what you see as a typical UFO.
Compare diagrams with other students. Were they similar? Why/Why not?

## LISTENING 😐

### Kidnapped by Aliens

Some people claim that they have been kidnapped by aliens. Travis Walton is one of them. In 1975 Walton was working in the forest with five other men. Their boss stopped the truck they were travelling in when they saw what was reported to be a flying saucer 5m above the trees. Walton jumped out and ran towards it. The others panicked and drove off. When they returned, Walton and the object had gone. There was a huge search for him. Five days later Walton turned up talking of capture by an alien race. Listen to extracts from Walton's statement and answer these questions.

*a* Why did he run towards the UFO?
*b* What happened when he approached the light?
*c* Describe what Walton saw.
*d* What happened at the end of the story.

*Glossary*

**hangar:** large shed where aircraft are kept

## TALKING POINT

Work individually and prepare an alternative explanation of Walton's story.

Share your ideas in a small group. Are any of the explanations more believable than Walton's story? Why/Why not? Do you believe Walton's story? Why/Why not?

## READING

If UFOs are regular visitors, then aliens may have visited the world in the past. *Streetwise* looks at some of the evidence. Read the text and answer the questions.

### DID EXTRATERRESTRIALS VISIT THE EARTH IN THE DISTANT PAST?

The idea that ancient astronauts might have visited the Earth first became popular when *Chariots of the Gods?* was published in English in 1969. The author, Erich von Daniken claims spaceships were observed in Mesopotamia thousands of years ago. The astronauts returned later to reveal the secrets of metal making, agriculture and written language. In support of his theories von Daniken points out that the mythologies of almost every culture include tales of winged animals and flying devices, and shows how ancient drawings and inscriptions are similar to modern astronauts. He also argues that many ancient achievements and mysteries, ranging from the building of the great pyramid in Egypt to the strange markings on the plain of Nazca, were only possible with the help of astronauts.

Von Daniken has been attacked by many scholars. For example, they argue that techniques used in the construction of the pyramids are now well known. His interpretation of early drawings and sculptures has also been attacked. Would interstellar space travellers really turn out to look like modern astronauts? Moreover, if the Earth was visited by extraterrestrials in the very early days of our species, the cultural impact must have been major – unless the extraterrestrials had the common sense not to interfere too much with whatever level of civilization then existed.

Von Daniken is, however, not alone. Robert Temple, in *The Sirius Mystery* (1976), examined anthropologists' reports about the Dogon tribe in North Africa. His analyses suggested that the Dogon knew that the planets of the Solar System went around the Sun in ellipses, rather than circles; they knew also that the dwarf-star companion of Sirius existed and was made up of very compressed matter. The Dogon were also aware that the planet Saturn had rings and that the planet Jupiter had four moons. These are pieces of information that cannot be discovered without a telescope – something that the Dogon have yet to invent, and Temple argues that the tribe was founded by spacemen from the companion of Sirius.

However, there are question marks. For example, Jupiter has more than four moons, and although Saturn does have spectacular rings we now know that Jupiter, Uranus and Neptune also have them. Why wasn't this mentioned by the visitors from outer space? As the first investigations of the Dogon did not take place until the 1930s or 1940s, it is far more likely that scientific information was passed on by explorers and missionaries who visited in the early twentieth century. After all, Sirius' companion was discovered in 1915.

Despite the lack of evidence and the shaky facts, theories like von Daniken's are still very popular. This is probably because he raises two fundamental mysteries – the wonders of human achievement, and the existence of life in outer space. While these remain of interest to us, von Daniken and others like him will continue to sell millions of books.

1 Summarize the main arguments in favour of the idea that Earth was visited by extraterrestrials in the past.
2 Summarize the main arguments against.
3 Why are books like *Chariots of the Gods?* so popular?
4 What is your personal view?

## VOCABULARY

1 Match the definitions to the words as they are used in the text.

| a | reveal | doubtful or weak |
|---|---|---|
| b | in support of | explanation of |
| c | interpretation of | varying between |
| d | ranging from | very great |
| e | common sense | not enough information or proof |
| f | impact | make known |
| g | major | natural ability to make good judgements |
| h | lack of evidence | effect |
| i | shaky | as evidence for |

2 What is the meaning of the prefixes in *italics*?

a *extra*terrestrials
b *astro*nauts
c *inter*stellar

**Passives**

1 Why is the passive used in these examples?
*Chariots of Fire was published in 1969 . . .*
*Spaceships were observed in Mesopotamia . . .*

2 Complete these with an appropriate form of the passive.
a He thinks Earth _____ (visit) by aliens many years ago.
b A team to investigate UFOs _____ just _____ (form).
c The Dogon scripts _____ (study) at the moment.
d I believe life _____ (discover) in outer space soon.

3 What is the rule for forming the passive?

### PRACTICE

1 Change the sentences from active to passive.
a Someone gave the Dogon information about Saturn.
The Dogon _____ .
b Von Daniken wrote *Chariots of the Gods?*
*Chariots of the Gods?* _____ .
c The New York Times published his ideas.
His ideas _____ .
d Someone had told the Dogon about Jupiter.
The Dogon _____ .
e Nobody believed me when I said that I had seen a UFO.
I _____ .
f Someone helped them to build the pyramids.
They _____ .
g They photographed him before his trip.
He _____ .

2 Expand the following to make sentences about Walton's experience.
a Walton capture/aliens in 1975.
b He take on board/spaceship.
c He put on a table/alien creatures.
d He take/another room/a man in blue.
e Something/put/his face.
f He release five/later.

### WRITING

*Streetwise* is interested in hearing from readers who have been kidnapped by aliens. Write a serious, or not so serious, account of what happened to you, where you were taken, what the aliens looked like, etc.

# RIGHT TO BE LEFT

## *WARM-UP*

### Part A

Which hand do you normally use in these tasks?

a   Writing
b   Drawing
c   Throwing
d   Using scissors
e   Using a toothbrush
f   Using a knife (without a fork)
g   Using a spoon
h   When you strike a match, which hand do you hold the match with?
i   When you open a jar, which hand do you use to hold the lid?

### Part B

1   Draw the profile of a dog or a horse.
2   Draw a circle with your right hand and mark an arrow to show the direction in which you drew the circle. Do the same with your left hand.
3   Close your eyes. Imagine that you're locked in a room, seated in a chair, with your hands tied behind you. In front of you is a telephone, your only means of rescue. Which foot do you use to pull the telephone closer.

Share your results with your partner before reading the text.

## *READING*

### GET IT RIGHT!

Most people believe that we are either left- or right-handed. This is incorrect. Chances are that you are more nearly ambidextrous than you realize. You can, for example, probably write quite well with your left hand even if you have always been right-handed.

The answers to the quiz should reveal which of you tends to be left-handed. In Part A, the more tasks you do with your left hand the more left-handed you are. In Part B you need to consider your results. In the first task, right-handers almost always draw the profile facing left. Left-handers draw it facing right.

When it comes to drawing circles, right handers will generally draw both circles in an

anti-clockwise direction. If you drew either circle clockwise, you probably have left-handed tendencies. If both were drawn clockwise, you are almost certainly left-handed.

Most people are right-footed, as well as right-handed and right-eyed. If you're right-handed and you imagined reaching out with your left foot you can consider yourself a mixed dominant or a frustrated left-hander.

Answer the questions.

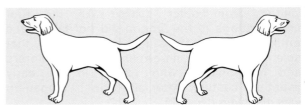

1   Which of the profiles above indicates that the drawer was left-handed?
2   Were the circles almost certainly drawn by a left- or right-hander? Why?
3   After having done the quiz and read the text do you agree that most of us are 'nearly ambidextrous'? Why/Why not?

## *LISTENING*

Imagine that you are suddenly in a world where everything is reversed. Door knobs are in the wrong place. Handles on tin-openers are on the wrong side and turn the wrong way. In fact millions of people who are left-handed face these problems every day because they live in a right-handed world.

What is it like being left-handed in a right-handed world? And what should be done about the left-handers' problems?

Share your answers, then listen to a report from Andrea Lynch.

1   Complete this table.

*Glossary*

**a mixed dominant:** someone who regularly uses both their left and right hand but not equally

|  | Problem | Solution |
|---|---|---|
| salutes and handshakes | people usually ____ | entitle left-handers to ____ |
| scissors | difficult to cut because: a ____ b ____ | give them ____ |
| writing | natural to write from ____. | change the way ____ |
| rulers | ____ | ____ |

## 2 Listen again and answer these questions.

a What percentage of people are left-handed?

b What are the two reasons suggested for right-hand bias?

c What are some of the advantages of being left-handed?

## Improve your wordpower

Complete the sentences with an appropriate word from this list.

*reverse   forwards   anti-clockwise
upwards   sideways   opposite
clockwise   backwards   downwards*

a Words like *level* and *noon* are palindromes. They read ____ as well as ____ .

b ⌐Լⱻ⅃ is an example of ____ writing.

c You can buy left-hand clocks which run ____ , the natural direction for left-handers. Normal clocks run in the ____ direction.

d The handle of a normal pencil sharpener turns in a ____ direction.

e Writing in English moves ____ , from left to right, rather than ____ or ____ .

## Improve your grammar

### Passive structures for modals

Modal verbs like *must, can, could, may, might, will, would, shall, should,* and *ought to,* can all be used in the passive.

The form is modal + passive infinitive:
*It must be done.*
*He ought to be invited.*

Or modal + perfect passive infinitive:
*He might have been hurt.*

## PRACTICE

1 Rewrite these sentences in the passive. Start with the word provided.

a Someone must do it.
It _____ .

b Someone can help him.
He _____ .

c They might build a new swimming pool.
A _____ .

d Someone might give him a chance.
He _____ .

e They ought to have punished her.
She _____ .

f They should have helped her find a job.
She _____ .

g You must clean this room.
This _____ .

2 Many countries have a Bill of Rights that sets out the things that people are entitled to. The tape suggested that left-handers should have a 'Bill of Lefts' which sets out their rights. One of these was:
*Left-handers should be entitled to use their dominant hand to shake hands and salute.*
Write five other statements.

## GETTING STREETWISE!   ☹

### Expressing reservations

Do you think left-handers should have a Bill of Rights? Why/Why not? Now listen to some young people discussing this question.

1 Summarize their points of view. Do any of them agree with you?

2 Listen again. This time write down the expressions used to express reservations and add them to this list.

The trouble is . . .
That may be so, but . . .
I'm still not sure . . .

## Use and Usage

### Prepositions with *agree*

We normally *agree with* someone. We *agree to* (do) something. In the sense of 'come to an arrangement', we find *about* (*Let's agree about that.*) and *on* (*We've agreed on a price.*), although *on* is sometimes omitted (*We've agreed a price.*).

Complete these examples with *to, with, about* or *on*.

a Do you agree ____ him about this?

b I agreed ____ see him.

c We have agreed ____ a name for our new group.

d She had agreed ____ let me borrow her bicycle.

e The company has not yet agreed ____ a new president.

# WHAT IS YOUR REACTION TIME?

## WARM-UP

Your reaction time is the speed at which the human body can react to a stimulus.

Discuss these questions in small groups.

a   Look at the pictures here and on the cover of this issue. What stimulus are the people reacting to, and why is reaction time crucial to their success?

b   How good do you think your own reaction time is? Why?

c   Why do people differ in their ability to react to stimuli?

## WRITING 1

Work in pairs.

1   Look at this picture. It shows some young people carrying out an experiment to measure reaction time. Discuss how the experiment works. Use the *Improve your writing* notes to help you write a set of instructions.

2   Exchange instructions with another pair and do exactly what their instructions tell you. If necessary, modify and improve the instructions.

3   Now check your answers by listening to someone reading their version of the instructions.

4   Carry out the experiment and note your results in this table.

| | Distance travelled by ruler | |
| | Me | My partner |
| --- | --- | --- |
| Trial 1 | | |
| Trial 2 | | |
| Trial 3 | | |
| Trial 4 | | |

5   Add the missing words to complete this short report of what you did.

Aim: To measure _____ .
Materials: _____ .
Method: We took turns to be _____ . The ruler _____ by the tester in a _____ position so that the zero mark was _____ the _____ . The ruler was released by the _____ and each time the distance _____ was _____ .
Results: See table.
Conclusion: My reaction time was _____ than my partners.

## Improve your wordpower

1   All these verbs and expressions are very useful for giving instructions. Can you show what they mean?

| | | | |
| --- | --- | --- | --- |
| pour | chop | tighten the top | fold |
| stir | slice | loosen the top | measure |
| tie | screw | spread | filter |

2   Complete these sentences with an appropriate form of some of the verbs. Use a different word in each one.

a   The liquid _____ into a bottle.

b   The leaf _____ into two pieces so that he could study it.

c   He _____ the top of the bottle so that the liquid could not escape.

d   _____ the liquid to remove the dirt.

e   _____ the string into a bow.

## Improve your writing

### Instructions and reports

**1** Successful written instructions are always clear and simple.

**a** Use headings for different sections. Here are some useful headings for telling someone how to do an experiment:

*Aim or title   Materials   Method Things to watch out for*

If we were telling someone how to cook something our headings might include:

*Ingredients   Method*

**b** Check that the instructions are complete.

**c** Use appropriate verb forms.

*Hold the ruler . . .*
*The tester releases the ruler . . .*
*After this has been done . . .*

**d** Use linking expressions such as:

*First/next/after that/etc.*

**e** If we are writing a scientific report we can use these headings:

*Aim   Materials   Method or Procedure   Results   Conclusions*

**2** Reports often use the passive because it is impersonal, especially in a formal style.

*The measurements were taken several times.*

## PRACTICE

**1** Rewrite these instructions using the passive.
Example
Add the liquid slowly.
*The liquid was added slowly.*

**a** Repeat the experiment several times.
**b** Form the students into a group.
**c** Use a stop watch to measure the time taken to react.
**d** Calculate the time taken to react by using a special formula.
**e** Add the ingredients gradually.
**f** Record the results in a table.
**g** Give a ruler to each pair.

**2** Use a mixture of active and passive forms to report what happened in these pictures.

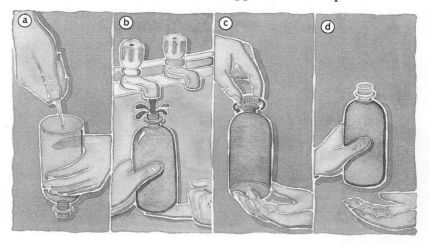

**3** Write the instructions so that someone else can do the experiment.

## TALKING POINT

Read the introduction before discussing each of the questions in a small group.

It is possible to measure the speed at which the human body reacts to the stimulus of touch with nothing more than a stop-watch. The best way to do this is for the students to stand in a circle and hold hands. They will then pass a squeeze around the circle and it then becomes possible to measure the time it takes for the squeeze to pass around the circle. The reaction time for one person can then be calculated.

Your aim is to produce instructions for carrying this experiment out successfully. Apart from the basic information you need to consider these questions.

**a** What size should the group be?
**b** How can students be prevented from anticipating the squeeze and reacting too soon?
**c** How can the time for the squeeze to pass around the circle be measured?
**d** Who will start the squeeze and how?
**e** Which direction should the squeeze pass in?
**f** How many trials should be made and how should the results be shown?
**g** How should the average reaction time per person be calculated?

Choose a secretary and be ready to present your instructions to the class. Vote for the best one and do the experiment!

## WRITING 2
Write a report of the experiment.

# A QUESTION OF CULTURE

## READING

Complete this quiz in pairs or small groups.

**1** Answer the questions.

**a** Britain or Great Britain is the largest island in Europe. What does Britain consist of?
**b** What does the United Kingdom consist of?
**c** Name two major British political parties.
**d** What does the abbreviation 'MP' stand for?
**e** When is Valentine's Day? How do people celebrate it?
**f** What do the Scots celebrate on 'hogmanay'?
**g** What is 'bed and breakfast'?
**h** What is Big Ben?
**i** Where is Oxford Street, and what is it famous for?
**j** What are public schools?
**k** When do people do A levels?

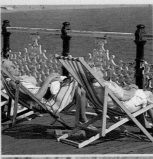

**2** Which aspects of British life are shown in the photographs?

**3** Decide if these statements about life in Britain are true or false.

**a** People who are invited to parties often take a bottle of something to drink with them.
**b** People shake hands with each other every time they meet.

**c** A napkin should be placed across the knees and never tucked into your front.
**d** One influential newspaper is printed on pink paper.
**e** Young people who are under 18 cannot drink alcohol in pubs.
**f** Most professional football matches are played on Saturday afternoon.
**g** People go to school six days a week.

## TALKING POINT

**1** Divide the questions in the quiz into groups and give each group a label (e.g. geography, tourism). Which group did you do best on? Why?

**2** How do people in your country view Britain and the British?
Work together and make a list of the positive and negative characteristics of the British as seen by the majority of people you know.

### Research

*Aims:*

**1)** to write a report on an aspect of the British or life in Britain. Option: Include a comparison with your own country.

**2)** to share the information so that your class increases its knowledge of life in Britain.

### *Hot tips!*

- Set clear objectives for your investigation and write this out in the form of a simple statement e.g. *My aim is to compare table manners in Britain with table manners in my country.*
- Consider possible sources of information. Sources may include:
  Books about Britain
  The reference section of the British Council or British Embassy
  British Tourist Association leaflets
  People who have been to or lived in Britain
- Decide on how you will present your findings, e.g. a poster, a written report, a recording, etc.

# STREETWISE
## ISSUE 6

## LEADERS

## I WISH I WERE . . .

## WORDS OF WISDOM

What shall I do?

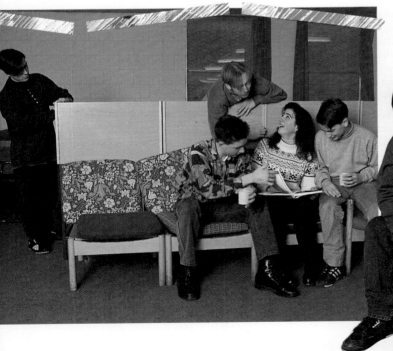

# LEADERS

## WARM-UP

1 Make a list of six of the written or unwritten rules you follow in everyday life.

Example
*You shouldn't talk when other people are talking.*

Share your list with the class and see if any of the rules appeared in more than one list.

## READING 📼

*Lord of the Flies* by William Golding is a classic of English Literature. Following a plane crash, a group of boys find themselves on a tropical island. In this extract from the beginning of the book, the boys decide what to do next.

### FOLLOW THE LEADER

Ralph cleared his throat.

'Well then.'

All at once he found he could talk fluently and explain what he had to say. He passed a hand through his hair and spoke.

'We're on an island. We've been on the mountain-top and seen water all round. We saw no houses, no smoke, no footprints, no boats, no people.'

Jack broke in.

'All the same you need an army – for hunting.'

'There aren't any grown-ups. We shall have to look after ourselves.'

The meeting hummed and was silent.

'And another thing. We can't have everybody talking at once. We'll have to have 'Hands up' like at school.'

He held the conch before his face and glanced round the mouth.

'Then I'll give him the conch.'

'Conch?'

'That's what this shell's called. I'll give the conch to the next person to speak. He can hold it when he's speaking.'

'But –'

'Look –'

'And he won't be interrupted. Except by me.'

Jack was on his feet.

'We'll have rules!' he cried excitedly. 'Lots of rules. Then when anyone breaks 'em –'

*Glossary*

**cradling:** holding something carefully in a hollow formed by your hands or arms

**'em:** short form of *them* (very informal)

**Where we was going to:** a grammatical error of the kind that is sometimes made in speech

**'cos:** short form of *because* (very informal)

'Whee-oh!'

'Wacco!'

'Bong!'

'Doink!'

Ralph felt the conch lifted from his lap. Then Piggy was standing cradling the great cream shell and the shouting died down. Jack, left on his feet, looked uncertainly at Ralph who smiled and patted the log. Jack sat down. Piggy took off his glasses and blinked at the assembly while he wiped them on his shirt.

'You're hindering Ralph. You're not letting him get to the most important thing.'

He paused effectively.

'Who knows we're here? Eh?'

'They knew at the airport.'

'My dad.'

Piggy put on his glasses.

'Nobody knows where we are,' said Piggy. He was paler than before and breathless. 'Perhaps they knew where we was going to; and perhaps not. But they don't know where we are 'cos we never got there.' He gaped at them for a moment, then swayed and sat down. Ralph took the conch from his hands.

'That's what I was going to say,' he went on 'when you all, all . . .' He gazed at their intent faces. 'The plane was shot down in flames. Nobody knows where we are. We may be here a long time.'

Nobody said anything.

*a* Which of the boys seems to be the leader?
*b* Why did the boys go silent at certain points of the meeting?
*c* What rule did they decide on for the group?
*d* Why did the boys get excited when Jack told them they would need lots more rules?

## VOCABULARY

Find words or phrases in the text which mean:

*a* made a short quick sound like a cough in order to make it easier to speak or in order to attract attention
*b* smoothly, with no hesitation or mistakes
*c* made a steady continuous noise
*d* became quieter
*e* hit lightly with his fingers
*f* shut his eyes and opened them again quickly
*g* making it more difficult for
*h* stopped speaking for a short time
*i* looked at them with an open mouth
*j* leaned slowly to one side and then another
*k* fixed, absorbed, and paying great attention

## TALKING POINT

Form small groups and try to sit in a circle. Choose an object which will function as a conch and place it in the centre. If you wish to speak, pick up the object and put it on your lap. When you have finished return the object to the centre. Take turns to discuss these questions.

1  What problems would a group of boys living alone on a desert island have to face? What solutions would you offer?
2  If you were in the same situation as these boys, what 'rules' would you have? How could you make sure you enforced them?

### Grammar quiz

**Conditionals with *if* and *unless***

1  Rewrite this sentence starting with *if*.
    *Unless you have the conch, you can't speak.*
    What is the meaning of *unless*?

2  *What would you do if you were living on the island?* Why do we use *would* in the question rather than *will*?

## PRACTICE

1  Put in *if* or *unless*.
a  They won't survive _____ they have water.
b  They will fight _____ they don't have rules.
c  You can't speak _____ you don't have the conch.
d  Piggy can't see _____ he wears glasses.

2  Complete each sentence so that it means the same as the sentence printed before it.
a  She won't win the election, if we don't help.
    Unless _____ .
b  Unless we change the rules, she'll leave.
    If _____ .
c  We couldn't live there without water.
    Unless _____ .
d  I wouldn't help her if she didn't change.
    Unless _____ .

3  Rewrite these, starting with the word in brackets and keeping the same meaning.
a  Finish your homework. You can't watch the match until you do! (Unless ...)
b  You can go out. But make sure you are back by eleven. (If ...)
c  I wouldn't go without a ticket. (Unless ...)
d  Work hard, or you won't get anywhere in life. (If ...)

## PRONUNCIATION

**Contrastive stress**

1  Listen and mark the main stress in B's answers.
a  A  She'll leave if we change the rules.
    B  No, she'll leave unless we change them.
b  A  He'll leave unless we change the rules.
    B  No, she'll leave unless we change them.
c  A  She'll stay if we don't change the rules.
    B  No, she'll leave unless we change them.

2  Why is a different word stressed in each answer?
3  Listen again and repeat. Then practise with a partner.

### Improve your wordpower

Match the people to what they are normally in charge of.

conductor       ship/aircraft
captain         a government department
head teacher    orchestra
caretaker       building
minister        school

## LISTENING

*Lord of the Flies* is a terrifying story of what happens when the normal rules of our society break down. It is often said that school is responsible for our socialization by teaching us the basic rules and skills we need to live with other people. But what should the role of teachers be? Should they teach children to question everything or to accept what is told to them? Listen to a story about an unusual teacher and answer these questions:

a  What was the cattywampus?
b  Why did everyone fail the test?
c  Why did Mr Whitson tell the story of the cattywampus?
d  Why do you think the primary school teacher was appalled about the story of Mr Whitson? Do you agree with him?

## WRITING

Write a letter to the Editor of *Streetwise* giving your views of Mr Whitson's approach to teaching.

# I WISH I WERE . . .

## WARM-UP

**Imitation is the sincerest form of flattery.**

*a* What do you feel about people who try to be like someone famous?

*b* How would you feel if lots of people wanted to imitate you?

## READING

1 Complete the text using the words and expressions in the box.

> style   insult   if   having   compliment
> for   to   when   wanting   and
> until   but   really   I suppose   exactly
> I just think   her own

### MATTER OF OPINION

**Is imitation really so flattering?**

To be called a copy-cat in the school playground is considered an _____ (a). But _____ (b) people you know well tell you that they like your new jeans and then buy exactly the same _____ (c) at least you know it wasn't empty praise. So should you feel pleased, or is this the kind of _____ (d) you could do without.

**I think we all imitate our friends a bit**, says Julie, 18 'If I've had a good idea about where to go _____ (e) a weekend or found a great new shampoo I'm only too happy _____ (f) share these things. If I turn up at a party _____ (g) find my friend dressed _____ (h) like me I actually feel more confident. _____ (i), 'What great taste we've both got.'

**There's nothing more irritating**, says Sheila 17. 'I have a friend who always copies my clothes and haircuts. I wish she wouldn't. She has no ideas of _____ (j) - it's pathetic!'

**I suppose I should feel flattered, but actually it makes me cross**, says Peter 18. 'Recently I was given a flashy new bike and was feeling _____ (k) pleased with myself - _____ (l) my friend rushed out and bought the same model. _____ (m) there's always going to be a bit of rivalry between friends _____ (n) it's nice to feel one step ahead.'

**It depends on what they're copying**, says Bill, 16. 'I was quite pleased _____ (o) my best friend decided to take Spanish at the same

*Glossary*

**It's pathetic!:**
expression used to show disapproval – someone or something is so bad or weak that it makes you feel angry (informal)

evening class because I like _____ (p) someone I know in class. But if he started _____ (q) everything that I have in life, I know it would drive me crazy.'

2 Place Julie, Sheila, Peter and Bill somewhere on this scale. Where would you place yourself? Why?

> Most in favour of being imitated ←→ Least in favour of being imitated

## VOCABULARY

Find words and phrases in the text that mean:

*a* someone who copies your behaviour, etc.
*b* approval/compliment that has no real value
*c* arrive
*d* annoying
*e* rather angry
*f* smart, bright and expensive
*g* active competition between people
*h* makes me mad/very angry

---

*Improve your grammar*

### Wish . . . would

*Wish . . . would* expresses a wish for a change in how someone else behaves:

*I wish you would be more polite.*
*I wish she wouldn't copy my hairstyle.*

We use the same pattern to express a wish for someone to do something, or for something to happen.

*I wish you would tell me the news.*
*I wish that dog would stop barking.*

### Wish + simple past tense

*Wish* and *If only* with a simple past verb express a wish for the present situation to be different.

*I wish I lived in New York.* (but I don't)
*If only I had a CD player.* (but I haven't)

With the verb *be* we can use *was* or *were* for 1st and 3rd person forms. *Were* is more formal than *was*.

*I wish I were Elvis.* (but I'm not)
*If only I was taller, I could play in the basketball team.* (but I'm not, so I can't)
*My room is very small. I wish it was bigger.* (NOT I wish my room would be bigger.)

## PRACTICE

1 Imagine that you are the people in these situations and make sentences with *I wish* + *simple past* or *I wish* + *would* for each of these situations.

a Alan is miserable because everyone else has new trainers but he hasn't.
b Alison read in the papers that they are still killing elephants. She wants them to stop.
c Alex works in a factory. He hates his job.
d Maria wants a job in a hotel but they want someone who speaks German. She can't.
e Peter is a painter but he wants to be a famous singer.
f Max is a farmer. The weather is hot and dry and it hasn't rained in months.
g Zena wants to be able to play the guitar.
h Helena smokes thirty cigarettes a day. She wants to give up.

2 Complete these sentences.

a I wish I had . . .
b I wish I were . . .
c If only I could . . .
d I wish it were Sunday because. . .
e I wish my best friend would . . .
f If only people wouldn't . . .

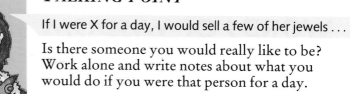

## *Improve your wordpower*

1 Match the sentences to the cartoons. You can use more than one sentence with some of the cartoons.

a I wish I could *drop out.*
b If I don't *get through* this time, I'll have to do them again.
c I wish I could *get out of* doing the dishes.
d I wish I could *keep up with* them. They walk so fast.
e If only we could *do away with* housework, there would be more time for having fun!

2 Match these definitions to the verbs in *italics* above.

abolish, withdraw from a group or society, pass an exam, go at the same speed as, avoid (a responsibility or duty)

## TALKING POINT

*If I were X for a day, I would sell a few of her jewels . . .*

Is there someone you would really like to be? Work alone and write notes about what you would do if you were that person for a day.

Read your notes to a small group without mentioning who you would like to be, and see if the other students can guess who you chose. When you have done this list all the disadvantages of being the people you chose.

## GETTING STREETWISE!

**Surprise and disbelief**

1 The following expressions can all be used to express surprise and disbelief. Do you have equivalent expressions in your language? What intonation would you use?

No! Never! You're joking. Gosh! You're pulling my leg. That's amazing. I don't believe it. Really? Wow!

2 Listen and repeat with an appropriate intonation.

3 Complete these extracts with a suitable expression from the list above.

*Extract 1*
A There is this guy who claims he saw Elvis in a petrol station.
B _____ .
A No, I'm not. He really claims to have seen him.
B Well, _____ .
A Neither do I.

*Extract 2*
A Did you know that Macaulay Culkin earned over $5 million for the sequel to *Home Alone*?
B _____ .
A It's true, and he was only eleven years old when he started making the film.
B _____ .

*Extract 3*
A Mike's just returned the CD he borrowed last year.
B _____ .
A He has!
B Well, that's incredible. I never thought I would see it again.

4 Now listen to a possible answer and repeat with the same intonation.

5 In pairs, write and perform your own mini-dialogue using these expressions.

# WORDS OF WISDOM

## *WARM-UP*

These extracts from letters to *Streetwise* are all from people who suffer badly from the same problem. Read the extracts before discussing the questions in small groups.

> When I see an item of clothing in a shop, I am afraid to go in and buy it. Every time I try to go into a shop I get embarrassed and hot. I always think the assistants in there are thinking 'Nothing in this shop would ever suit them.'
>
> Alex

> I know some people who can't talk because of shyness. My problem is completely opposite - I cannot stop talking because of it. You see, if a member of the opposite sex comes to talk to me, instead of going quiet I chat like mad.
>
> Chris

> I am the world's most boring person and I never go anywhere. I have no self-confidence and try not to talk to people.
>
> Sally

*a* What problem are they suffering from?
*b* What are the symptoms and how does it affect people?
*c* Why does it affect some people more than others?

## *LISTENING* 😦

You are going to hear an expert answering the questions you have been discussing.

1 Listen and see how far he agrees with you.
2 Complete this summary.
- Don't feel bad about ____ ____ .
- If you feel shy talking to people, try ____ them ____ .
- Try not to ____ ____ from situations that make you ____ . Get a ____ to give moral support.
- List your ____ ____ .
3 Re-read the letters in the warm-up. Is anything that you have heard particularly appropriate to the writers? If so, what?

## *Improve your writing*

### Advice

Here are some guide-lines for giving advice in writing.

1 Decide on your audience. What do they already know about the topic? Is it someone you know or a group of strangers? Aim for an informal, friendly style.
2 Make sure that any advice you give is clear by starting with a sentence outlining the problem.
3 Choose appropriate expressions to introduce your piece of advice. (Those with asterisks are more formal than the others.)

### Advising someone to do something

*If I were you I would . . .*
*It would be a good idea if . . .\**
*Unless you do this, you won't . . .*
*You ought to . . .*
*Perhaps you should . . .\**

### Advising against something

*Whatever you do, don't . . .*
*Never listen . . .*
*It's best not to . . .\**
*You shouldn't . . .*

## *PRACTICE*

1 This is a reply to the letter from Sally. Put the sentences in the best order.

*a* They might even think you don't like them.
*b* It helps to put them at their ease.
*c* If I were you I would start smiling and talking to people.
*d* It is by no means true that you are the most boring person in the world.
*e* That is your defence against having to meet new people.
*f* As soon as you do this they will respond.
*g* If necessary tell people you are shy.
*h* Unless you do this people will think you are cold.
*i* If you follow this advice, you will soon discover that other people can be boring too.
*j* Yours,
*k* Dear Sally,

**2** Complete the missing sections of this letter. Put one word in each space.

Dear Alex,

    I have the same ____ (*a*), I don't like going into ____ (*b*) either.

    If I ____ (*c*) you I would start by going ____ (*d*) shops and just looking around. ____ (*e*) doesn't matter if you ____ (*f*) out without buying anything. ____ (*g*) you are comfortable with being in ____ (*h*) shop you can ask questions ____ (*i*) hold clothes up to your body. Finally, you ____ (*j*) be able to try things on. Perhaps you ____ (*k*) take a friend as well. This ____ (*l*) shopping easier and you will have moral ____ (*m*).

**3** Write a reply to Chris's letter.

## *Improve your wordpower*

**1** What is the difference between *advice* and *advise*?

**2** What is the difference between *embarrassed* and *embarrassing*? Choose the correct form.

*a* I was so *embarrassed/embarrassing* that I went red.

*b* I find situations like this very *frightened/frightening*.

*c* Pop music is so *bored/boring*.

*d* His problem is very *worried/worrying*.

*e* Exams are *terrified/terrifying*.

*f* Were you *disappointed/disappointing* by what you saw?

*g* The news was *depressed/depressing*.

*h* My friends have been very *encouraged/encouraging* about my trip.

**3** Complete the table.

| Adjective | Abstract noun |
|-----------|---------------|
| shy | shyness |
| friendly | |
| tired | |
| happy | |
| weak | |

Now complete these sentences with nouns or adjectives from the table.

*a* Money did not bring him ____ .

*b* I hadn't eaten for days. I was ____ from hunger.

*c* ____ is not one of his qualities. He is always arguing with people.

*d* Do you suffer from ____ after a long day at school?

*e* He is so ____ that he goes red when someone enters a room.

## PRONUNCIATION 😐
### Word stress

**1** Here are some word families. Mark the main stress and examples of the sound /ə/.

| Verb | Adjective | Noun |
|------|-----------|------|
| embarrass | embarrassed/ embarrassing | embarrassment |
| encourage | encouraged/ encouraging | encouragement |
| disappoint | disappointed/ disappointing | disappointment |

**2** Listen and check your answers.

**3** Listen and repeat.

## WRITING

Bullying, teasing and shyness often go together.

Work in a small group and discuss why some people are teased and bullied more than others. What happens to them? Why? What can they do about it? Should they stand up to the bullies and fight back? Should they get parents, teachers or friends to take action?

*a* Imagine that you are a victim of bullying. Write a letter in which you ask *Streetwise* for advice.

*b* Exchange letters with another group and write a reply in which you give the person advice on how to deal with their problem.

*c* Read out some of the letters and the answers. Vote for the best one.

# POLITENESS

## READING

### THANKS!!

Sometime ago, an Italian friend of mine made the following discovery during an afternoon shopping trip: in Britain you need four 'thank yous' to buy a bus ticket. The conductor comes up with his machine on his shoulders: he says the first 'thank you' (meaning 'I am here'). The passenger hands over the money with another 'thank you' (I can see you, here is the money). Another 'thank you' from the conductor (read: this is the correct change, the deal is struck, here is your ticket). At this point the passenger takes the ticket and utters an appropriate 'thank you'. You can total up to six 'thank yous' if you do not hand over the correct change. Italians are amused by this ritual; when they have to pay for their tickets at home they normally do it with a grunt. Americans, who normally carry out such transactions in silence, are flabbergasted.

From: *Inglesi* by Beppe Severgnini

This extract is from a best-selling portrait of the British by an Italian author. It highlights one of the features of the English language – the need to be polite.

1  Work with a partner and act out the buying of a ticket as described in the text.
2  How would the same transaction be carried out in your country?
3  Are there any forms of behaviour that make foreigners seem impolite, or even too polite, in your country?

## PLEASE AND THANK YOU

*Please* and *Thank you* are important expressions. Unfortunately, they are often misused. Here are some guide-lines:

a  *Please* is used with requests and orders.

   *Please stand over there.* (order)
   *Would you mind standing over there, please?* (polite request)

   Note that merely adding *please* does not change an order into a polite request.

b  *Please* is not used to ask people to repeat what they said. We say *Sorry?* or *What?* (informal) or *Pardon?* (formal) with a

rising intonation.

c  *Please* is not used to give things to people. Use *Here you are* or *There you are*.

d  *Please* is not used as an answer to *Thank you* or *Thanks*. Common answers are *Not at all* (formal), *It's a pleasure* (formal), *That's all right* (informal).

e  *Thank you* is often used to accept an offer (in the same way as *Yes, please*). We usually say *No, thank you* when we want to refuse. Compare:

   A  *Would you like a drink?*
   B  *Thank you.*
   A  *What would you like? Tea or coffee?*

   A  *Would you like a drink?*
   B  *No, thank you.*
   A  *Are you sure?*

1  How are the equivalents of *please* and *thank you* used in your language?

## LISTENING ☒

The use of polite formulae as well as expressions like *please* and *thank you* is half the battle. However, the tone and intonation we use are also crucial if we want to be polite. Listen to these examples. One of the speakers would sound impolite to a fluent English speaker in each case. Underline the part where the intonation is faulty and decide how you could make the speaker sound more polite in each case.

a  Air hostess: Would you like a drink?
   Passenger: No, thank you.
b  Child: Can I have an ice-cream, please?
   Ice-cream seller: Here you are.
c  Woman in canteen: What would you like?
   Man: I think I'd like the chicken, please.
   Woman: Sauce?
   Man: Er, no thanks.
d  Boy: Post this for me!
   Friend: Yes, of course.
e  Girl: Could you shut the door?
   Friend: Sure.

### Research

*Aim:*

1)  to produce a short leaflet explaining how to be polite in English or your own language.

### Glossary

**grunt:** low, rough sound from deep in the throat

**flabbergasted:** extremely surprised

# GRAMMAR REVIEW ISSUES 5 AND 6

## PASSIVE

### Form

The appropriate tense of *be* (e.g. *is, was, is being, have been*,etc.) + past participle (*made, seen, cleaned, written,* etc.)

| It | is | |
|---|---|---|
| | has been | |
| | was | |
| | was being | cleaned. |
| | had been | |
| | will be | |
| | is going to be | |

### Uses

1 When we do not know who or what does something.

2 When the 'doer' of the action is not important. This is quite common in scientific writing.

3 The use of *by* + the passive gives special emphasis to the 'doer'.

### Examples

*Two men have been killed in a bomb attack in Northern Ireland today. My car was stolen.*

*In the first experiment, subjects were given a small amount of tea.*

*This cake was made by my youngest brother. The Walkman was invented by a Japanese Company.*

### Notes

The passive is used in both spoken and written English, but it is probably more common in writing. It is often found in textbooks and reports as well as notices and announcements.

*The substance is weighed twice in order to...*
*Candidates are required to be present ten minutes before the exam starts.*
*Lunch will be served at 1pm.*

The passive is also common in news reports.
*A bomb exploded in the city centre yesterday, but luckily nobody was injured.*
*Twenty men were arrested after the football match.*

## PASSIVE STRUCTURES FOR MODALS

### Form

modal + passive infinitive, e.g. *It can't be done.*
modal + perfect passive infinitive, e.g. *It can't have been done.*

### Uses

*Can, could, must, may, might, will, would, shall, should, ought to* can all be used in the passive.

### Examples

*This car can be driven. He must have been here. He should be stopped. He might have been hurt.*

## SECOND CONDITIONAL

### Form

*if* + simple past + *would* + base form

### Uses

1 To talk about unreal or hypothetical present or future situations.

2 To talk about present or future situations that are not likely.

### Examples

*What would you do if you went to live on the island?*

*If I won a car, I would be thrilled.*

### Note

The choice between the first conditional (*if* + simple present + *will* + base form) and the second conditional depends on our view as to how likely or possible something is. We use the first conditional if we think something is likely, and the second conditional if we think it is not, so the second conditional is used for hypothetical situations. Compare:
*If I get Grade A in my English exam, I will be very pleased.* (= It is possible that I will get Grade A.)
*If I got Grade A in my English exam, I would be very pleased.* (= I think it is unlikely that I will get Grade A.)

## UNLESS

*Unless* + positive = *if* + negative

*Unless* usually means the same as *if* + negative. Compare:
*If you don't have the conch, you can't speak.*
*Unless you have the conch, you can't speak.*

But note that *unless* means 'except on the condition that' and it therefore cannot replace *if* in sentences like:
*I'll be surprised if he doesn't come.*

## WISH . . . WOULD

### Form

*wish* + object + *would* + base form

### Uses

1 To express a wish for a change in how someone behaves.

2 To express a wish for someone to do something, or for something to happen.

### Examples

*I wish she wouldn't copy my hairstyle.*
*I wish you would be more polite.*

*I wish you would tell me what the problem is.*
*I wish that dog would stop barking.*

### Note

If we want to express a wish for a change in our own behaviour, we use *I wish I could* + base form and not *I wish I would...*
*I wish I could stop smoking.*

## WISH + SIMPLE PAST

### Form

*wish* and *If only* + simple past

### Use

1 To express a wish for the present situation to be different. These wishes are generally impossible and therefore hypothetical.

### Examples

*I wish I were Elvis.*
*My room is very small. I wish it was bigger.*
*If only I was taller. I could play in the basketball team.*

### Notes

We can use *were* for first and second person forms. *Were* is more formal than *was*.

*I wish I were/was rich.*
*Liz wishes she were/was on holiday.*

We cannot use *would* in these types of wishes.

*I wish my room was bigger.* (NOT *I wish my room would be bigger.*)

We can use *could* in these types of wishes.
*I wish I could play the guitar, but I can't.*

## GRAMMAR PRACTICE

### A

1 Complete these sentences with an appropriate passive form of the verb in brackets.

Example
Romeo and Juliet *was written* (write) by William Shakespeare.

a I _____ (give) a watch for my last birthday.
b The stadium _____ (build) by this time next year.
c Oranges _____ (grow) in California.
d He told me his bike _____ (steal) during the night.
e I hope that a homework machine _____ (invent) soon.
f A lot of money _____ (spend) on education in recent years.
g These sweets _____ (make) in our town for centuries.
h We _____ (not told) the answers to the last test.

2 Complete the sentences using an appropriate form of the verbs in brackets: simple present, simple past, *will*, *won't*, *would(n't)*.

Example
I'*ll tell* (tell) your mother unless you stop.

a I _____ (help) if I could.
b I'll lend Peter the money if he _____ (need) it.
c Provided they had plenty to eat, they _____ (be) happy.
d Would you marry the prince if he _____ (ask) you.
e Unless Chris improves, she _____ (fail) the exam.
f If I _____ (be) you, I would go.

3 What would you say? Use *I wish...would/wouldn't* to write an appropriate sentence for each situation.

Example
Your brother plays very loud music while you are doing your homework.
*I wish you wouldn't play loud music while I'm doing my homework.*

a You are on a long walk. Your sister is walking very slowly.
b A friend has got you into trouble by talking to you in class again.
c One of the students in your class always speaks softly when he answers a question and you can't hear the answer.
d Your brother always borrows your favourite jacket when you want to wear it.

*e*   You are the only member of your family who remembers to feed your pet cat.

*f*   The person who shares your bedroom never tidies it and you always have to do it.

*g*   You really like hamburgers, but your mother never cooks them.

## B

**1**  Rewrite these sentences in the passive. Start with the word provided.

Example
Someone can tell him the good news.
He *can be told the good news.*

*a*   You must help her.
She _____ .

*b*   Someone might have told him.
He _____ .

*c*   Could someone invite him?
Could _____ .

*d*   They ought to have helped people who were in trouble.
People _____ .

*e*   I hope someone can invent a cure for cancer soon.
I hope a _____ .

*f*   Someone ought to prevent him from doing this.
He _____ .

**2**  The Streetwise panel had a discussion about the problems of tall people. Use the passive to report their opinions.

Example
'People shouldn't laugh at them'.
*They shouldn't be laughed at.*

*a*   'Someone should make longer beds.'

*b*   'We could open special clubs for tall people'.

*c*   'We needn't treat them specially.'

*d*   'We ought to give them special cars.'

*e*   'We should also help short people.'

*f*   'We can't give special treatment to all the minorities.'

**3**  Finish each of the sentences so that it means the same as the sentences printed before it.

*a*   Unless Sarah leaves soon she will miss her bus.
If _____ .

*b*   The match will be cancelled if the weather is bad.
Unless _____ .

*c*   I won't lend him the money unless he needs it.
If _____ .

*d*   I won't see him if he doesn't apologise.
I refuse _____ unless _____ .

*e*   Without our goalkeeper, we would lose more matches.
If _____ .

*f*   Unless anyone has questions, the lesson is over.
If _____ .

**4**  Add an appropriate end to each sentence.

Example
I am very shy. I wish *I were more confident.*

*a*   I can't ride a horse. If only _____ .

*b*   The weather is very hot! I wish _____ .

*c*   We don't have tickets for the concert. If only _____ .

*d*   Life is boring! I wish _____ .

*e*   I can't play baseball. If only _____ .

*f*   I don't like my hair. I wish _____ .

*g*   Maria doesn't get good marks. She wishes _____ .

**5**  Complete each sentence so that it means the same as the one before it.

Example
I want to be able to speak English fluently.
*I wish I spoke English fluently.*

*a*   I would like to help you but I can't.
I wish _____ .

*b*   He would like to be rich, but he's poor.
He wishes _____ .

*c*   He doesn't want you to copy his homework.
He wishes you _____ .

*d*   I would like to be at the beach right now and not in this exam.
I wish _____ .

*e*   I want them to be more helpful.
If only _____ .

## C

**1**  Imagine that you are part of a group living on a desert island. Use the passive form of modals such as *can*, *should*, *must*, *needs to be*, etc., to write down ten 'rights' or 'rules' which are essential if you are to live together peacefully.

Example
*Each person must be given enough food.*

**2**  Write a paragraph describing some of the things you would or wouldn't do if you went to live on your dream island.

**3**  Do your relatives do anything that really annoys you? Use *I wish + would*, *could*, *were*, etc. to list six of your major complaints.

Example
*I wish my aunt wouldn't always talk about what I was like when I was a baby.*

## REASONS FOR READING

Reading is a skill that is learnt over a period of time. Good readers read in different ways for different reasons.

1   Think about your reasons for reading in your own language. Do you read:
  - for entertainment – magazines, stories, novels, newspapers, etc?
  - to learn about a subject – for study, hobbies, etc?
  - to find a piece of information – e.g. a telephone number, a word in a dictionary, information from an encyclopedia, etc?
  - to follow instructions – e.g. recipes, games, etc? ·
  - to decide if something is worth looking at/going to/buying – publicity leaflets, adverts, brochures, etc?

2   How does your approach differ for each type of reading? Think about differences such as the length of time you spend reading, the speed at which you read, etc.

## HOW WE READ

We read differently according to our purpose.

For example, if we are looking for a piece of information such as someone's telephone number, we will scan the text and ignore most of the words because we know what we are looking for.

If we are looking for the general idea, we are likely to skim the text. This involves fast reading to get a surface view. Most people skim newspapers and magazines. If they find something interesting, they may stop and read it in more detail.

Intensive reading is what we do when we study. This is slower and more serious, and we may need to re-read some parts again to get a fuller understanding. This is in contrast with normal or light reading which is done by choice and where we do not need to worry about detail, e.g. reading a novel on the beach.

1   Decide if these statements are true or false.
a   There is only one way of reading.
b   When we read, we normally read every word.
c   When we read for pleasure, we do not worry about understanding every word or remembering what we have read.

## WHAT THE EXAMINER WANTS

Techniques for testing reading comprehension include:
  - questions about the text.
  - multiple-choice questions.
  - true/false questions.
  - questions where you need to complete a task (e.g. label a diagram).
  - extracts from a text that need to be put back in the correct position.
  - jumbled sentences or paragraphs that need to be put back into the correct order.
  - gaps in a text to complete with a single word or expression.

1   List the techniques used to test reading comprehension in any exam you may be preparing for.

## DOING BETTER IN READING EXAMS

Examiners normally aim to test a variety of reading skills so...

  - Start by looking at the questions to see what is required. Instructions like *Find...*, *Look for...*, will almost certainly require scanning, and it may be possible to do the task without reading the text in detail.
  - If not, skim the text to identify the sections which are likely to contain the answers. If appropriate, pencil in your answers but always check these carefully.
  - If there is no obvious answer in the text you may need to draw conclusions from the information that is there. For example, you can answer these questions about the text below even though none of the information is given directly.

    *Are the boys students?*
    *Where are they?*
    *Is Mr Williams a teacher?*
    *Is he strict?*

    *The boys sat laughing and playing while one of them cleaned the blackboard. However, when Mr Williams walked in, they all fell silent and stood up ...*

  - Use the context, any pictures or illustrations as well as clues within the text, such as titles, to help you build up meaning.
  - Finally, remember that you do not necessarily need to understand and process every word to get the details you need from a text.

1   Why should you read the questions before reading the text?

# STREETWISE

## ISSUE 7

## THE ART OF GETTING HITCHED QUICK

## ARE SCHOOLS UNFAIR TO GIRLS?

## THE WAY WE ARE

# THE ART OF GETTING HITCHED QUICK

## *WARM-UP*
Work in small groups and agree on what you would expect of a really romantic wedding.

## *READING*
Read the text and answer the questions.

### MARRIAGE JAPANESE STYLE

*The bride is wearing a stunning white silk kimono which costs a million yen for a day's rental. She is about to be married in a building which sells weddings – mass produced for the Japanese market, and complete to the last detail.*

Only fifty or sixty years ago, marriage in middle-class Japan was a very formal business. Matchmaking would be done by a go-between such as an aunt, a cousin or some local widow and potential brides would meet their potential grooms at an *omial*, or formal introduction.

Since the war, though, things have changed. People have moved to the cities, and can no longer rely on the methods which their grandparents used to find partners. For those who haven't met someone and fallen in love, there are specially arranged company parties to find possible mates in the same organisation, and dating agencies which offer computer-generated diagrams showing the customer how closely matched the other person on the mailing list is.

Once the date is set, many couples find they don't have enough time to worry about the details of a wedding. So companies have sprung up to provide a complete wedding service.

The building we are in does about sixteen marriages a day. The glass-walled control room has seven banks of switches, dials and television screens, each one the nerve-centre of a different wedding in a different room. The rooms are 'hotel style' with large gold-coloured velvet chairs and champagne-coloured carpets. Most customers choose a shinto ceremony. They then have to decide on the food they offer to their guests. The choice is simple: Japanese or French, and it is far from cheap. The total bill is two or three times the cost of the dinner because of the extras. These can include clothes-rental, photographs, music, drink, flowers, candles, the master of ceremonies, lasers, dry ice, and doves which the couple release on the way out. To record the event there is an in-house video service which uses up to three cameras simultaneously and the uniquely Japanese extras include gold-plated telephone cards, personalized with the guest's name, and the presents. These consist of presentation packs of sweets, biscuits, etc. to be given, not to the couple, but to each guest in return for the traditional gift of money in a special presentation envelope.

There is one economy available however, and this is in the form of the economy model wedding cake. From the edge of the hall it looks magnificent. Closer, it seems a bit dried up. The cake is made of plaster of Paris, and on the far side there is a block of creamy white sponge cake, ready to be cut out by the bride. The guests know exactly what is happening, and after the event they admit happily that the cake looked too beautiful to be real, but they do not mind. It is all part of a dream wedding!

1 Use your own words to describe how the pattern of finding a marriage partner has changed in Japan in recent years.
2 Why are people keen to use marriage service companies?
3 Identify the expressions used to convey the idea that the weddings which are being described are factory-like.

## *Glossary*

**shinto:** patriotic Japanese faith, which is a collection of beliefs and customs relating to nature worship and Japan's mythical past, but very much a part of modern life

**dry ice:** solid carbon dioxide gas ($CO_2$), used to keep things cold, or to produce smoke for theatrical effects

**plaster of Paris:** white paste that becomes very hard when dry, used to hold broken bones in place while they heal

## *VOCABULARY*
Find words and phrases in the text that mean:

*a* extremely beautiful and impressive
*b* amount of money that you pay to use something for a certain period of time
*c* made (or done?) in large quantities
*d* the activity of encouraging people to form relationships or get married
*e* appeared quickly
*f* happening at the same time

2 Which of these would you expect to see in a wedding in your country?
*a* presentation packs of sweets and biscuits
*b* a plaster of Paris wedding cake
*c* traditional gifts of money
*d* a video camera
*e* a master of ceremonies

## Grammar quiz

### too and enough

1 Insert either *too* or *enough*:
a *It looked _____ beautiful to be real.*
b *I wasn't walking quickly _____ to catch up with them.*
c *She was walking _____ quickly for me.*
d *She is old _____ to marry.*
e *They do not have _____ time.*

## PRACTICE 1

Rewrite these sentences so that they keep the same meaning.

a She isn't old enough to get married.
She's too _____ .
b I didn't have enough money for it all.
I had too _____ .
c She wasn't tall enough to reach the cake.
She was too _____ .
d I arrived too late to see the wedding.
I didn't _____ .

## Improve your grammar

### Sequence of adjectives
Look at these examples.

| opinion | size age shape | colour | origin | material | noun |
|---------|----------------|--------|--------|----------|------|
| stunning | large new | white gold | Japanese | velvet silk | kimono chairs |

General qualities come before particular ones.
*creamy white sponge cake*
Personal opinions go before more objective words.
*stunning white silk*
We usually use a maximum of two or three adjectives before the noun, adding extra details afterwards.
*gold-plated telephone cards, personalized with the guest's name*

## PRACTICE 2

1 Decide on the correct adjective order.
a French/expensive/menu
b silk/white/beautiful/wedding dress
c gold/wedding rings/matching/two
d attractive/name cards/pink
e embroidered/red/cushions/large/with the couple's name

2 Describe the people here and on the cover of this issue. Use groups of adjectives to describe what they are wearing and how they appear physically.

## PRONUNCIATION 😐

### /juːst/ and /juːzd/

In a phrase like *weddings used to be very formal* the verb *used to* is pronounced /juːst/.

In *Dry ice is used to produce smoke* the verb *used to* is pronounced /juːzd/. The adjective *used* /juːzd/ also features /z/.

1 Decide how the forms of *use* are pronounced in these examples.
a I used to know him.
b A car was used to go to the reception.
c This is a used car.
d He used to use another vehicle.

2 Listen to check your answers. Then listen again and repeat.

## LISTENING 😐

### Who's for a quick service?

You are going to listen to an interview with Charlotte Richards, the woman on the cover. In it she explains why she started a drive-in wedding parlour. Listen to what she says, and decide which of these statements is true according to what is said on the tape.

a In Las Vegas you can get married without leaving your car.
b You don't need a blood test to get married in Las Vegas.
c You don't need a marriage licence there.
d Weddings are cheap in Las Vegas.
e Drive-in weddings attract people who want to get married in private.
f Drive-in weddings are very popular.
g She feels drive-in weddings are less serious than church weddings.
h The service was started to make money.

# ARE SCHOOLS UNFAIR TO GIRLS?

## READING

Do you think girls would learn better in single sex schools? Why/Why not?

Now read the texts below and see if they support your ideas.

**A**

If exam results were the only important factor, girls and boys would invariably study at separate schools. In England, students from single-sex day schools achieved the best results at A level this year while at mixed boarding schools the pass rate was considerably lower. There was little difference between the sexes, with girls passing at a marginally better rate than boys.

However, these facts have not had any effect on the current trend – the numbers of girls joining traditionally male schools has doubled in the past ten years, and more parents and pupils are accepting mixed schooling.

**B**

Boys don't benefit from single sex schools. The more boys there are the more unruly and violent they are. Girls on their own do better in the subjects they avoid in a mixed school, such as science and maths. But the powers-that-be have decided that mixed schools are 'better'. It seems that keeping boys happy is far more important than encouraging girls to do well in education. And the way that a lot of boys keep themselves happy is by turning sexual attention on their female fellow pupils. 'Walk past a gang of boys in the corridors or outside, and you can hear them making loud comments about you.'

It is the same in the classrooms. If there isn't enough apparatus to go round in a science lesson, the boys grab it all and the girls hang back. In drama lessons, boys act out their ideas, with the girls as spectators or props.

When it comes to class discussion, boys commonly take up two-thirds of chat, even when there are fewer of them in the group. Another researcher found that in English groups, for every one girl who spoke up, there were four boys who did. For every girl who asked questions, there were two boys who did, and for every girl who was given praise or encouragement, three boys were patted on the back. You can't even say this was because the boys deserved it – girls do slightly better in all exam subjects.

**C**

Teachers may play a larger role than nature in differentiating between the sexes. Studies show they tend to favor boys by calling on them more often and pushing them harder. Myra and David Sadker, professors of education at American University have found that girls do better when teachers are sensitive to gender bias and refrain from sexist language, such as the use of 'man' to mean 'all of us'. Single-sex classes in math and science can also boost female performance by eliminating favoritism and male disapproval of female achievement.

Now answer the questions.

*a* Which of the texts comes from a magazine for teenage girls, which from a British newspaper and which from an American magazine? Give reasons for your answers.

*b* A number of arguments against mixed schools are presented in these texts. Which ones, if any, do you agree with? Which would you reject? Why?

## VOCABULARY

*1* What is the meaning of the expressions in **bold**. Give reasons for your answers.

*a* girls and boys would **invariably** study
  *i* always
  *ii* never

*b* the **pass rate**
  *i* the number of people who take an exam in a particular period
  *ii* the number of people who succeed in an exam in a particular period

*c* the current **trend**
  *i* general tendency or fashion
  *ii* movement downwards

*d* the more **unruly** and violent
  *i* difficult to control
  *ii* angry

*e* enough **apparatus**
  *i* set of instruments, etc. used in scientific experiments
  *ii* textbooks

*2* Rewrite the parts in **bold** so that you keep the same meaning.

*a* three boys **were patted on the back**
*b* the number ... has **doubled**
*c* **refrain from** using sexist language

---

### Glossary

**boarding school:** school where some or all of the pupils live during term time in contrast with a day school where the students go home at night

**powers-that-be:** way of referring to people in authority that you disapprove of

**props:** objects, furniture, etc that you use in a play

**gender bias:** prejudice directed at a person because of their sex

## Improve your grammar

### Modifying comparatives

Words like *very*, *too* and *quite* can modify adjectives but not comparatives.

*He's very old.* (NOT *He's very older.*)

To modify comparisons we can put a word or phrase (e.g. *slightly*, *a lot*) before a comparative to say how much quieter/better/more complicated/etc. something is.

*Are girls slightly better at exams than boys?*
*Girls are a lot quieter than boys.*

The expressions we can use before a comparative include:

*much, considerably, a lot, lots, far,* (= a large amount)
*marginally, a little, slightly, a bit.* (= a small amount)
*hardly any* (= very, very little)

## PRACTICE 1

1   Complete the sentences with the correct form of the adjectives in brackets.

a   The girls I know are ____ than the boys. (sophisticated)
b   He is a bit ____ than the other students. (bad)
c   She is considerably ____ than her sister. (young)
d   Her new school is a bit ____ than the old one so they will be able to save some money. (expensive)
e   He is much ____ than his brother. (clever)
f   My sister is much ____ than the rest of the family. (hard-working)

2   Use the table to make ten true sentences. Include some comparatives and subjects of your own.

| I | | slightly | shorter | |
|---|---|---|---|---|
| My best friend | am | marginally | more intelligent | |
| The boys in class | is | considerably | taller | than |
| The girls in class | are | hardly any | better behaved | |
| The team | was | much | quieter | |
| | were | a little | better looking | |
| | | a bit | better | |

## Use and usage

### *than me* and *than I am*

After *than* or *as*, a personal pronoun on its own has the object form (e.g. *me*).

*You're older than me.*
*He isn't as clever as her.*

But if the pronoun has a verb after it, then we use the subject form (e.g. *I*).

*You're older than I am.*
*He isn't as clever as she is.*

Put in the correct pronoun.
a   My friend Nick is a much better guitarist than ____ am but he has been playing longer than ____ .
b   I'm a better player than Margaret. I've scored more goals than ____ has.
c   You saw her play. Am I better than ____ ?

## TALKING POINT

Look at these questions before taking part in a debate on the motion

*Mixed schools should be abolished.*

Are girls often upset by the behaviour and comments of boys, both in and out of class?
In your experience, do girls take considerably less part in lessons than boys?
Are certain subjects seen as 'girls' subjects?
Do you think the presence of the opposite sex contributes to poorer academic performance?

## GETTING STREETWISE!  ☹

### Moans and groans

Is there anything that you really can't stand?

1   Listen to what some *Streetwise* readers had to say on the subject. Write down the expressions they used to introduce their moans.
2   List as many expressions for talking about your dislikes as you can.

## PRACTICE 2

Is there anything you really dislike about the opposite sex? Or school? Or the place you live?

1   List five of your personal dislikes.
2   Use the expressions you have just learnt to take part in a class survey of your pet hates.

# THE WAY WE ARE

## WARM-UP

1  Get into pairs. Start by working alone and make notes about your partner's:

- hobbies and interests
- tastes in fashion and music
- favourite sports and entertainment

   Take it in turns to read your notes to your partner and find out if you were right.

2  Now ask your partner:
   Do you feel you are a different person in different situations? For example, do you speak differently when you are with different people?

## LISTENING 😦

Now listen to how some *Streetwise* readers answered the question in task 2 of the *Warm-up* and answer the questions.

1  Match the speakers to the pictures. Be ready to give reasons.
2  Complete the grid.

| Thinks she/he | Sue | Digby | Justin | Maria |
|---|---|---|---|---|
| has a loud voice | | | | |
| speaks softly | | | | |
| has a posh accent | | | | |
| mumbles | | | | |
| speaks quickly | | | | |
| has a high-pitched voice | | | | |
| does not really change the way she/he speaks with friends and family | | | | |

3  Do you feel the same as any of the speakers? Why/Why not?

## TALKING POINT

Work through these questions in small groups.

1  These adjectives describe how people look:
   smart: well-dressed, neat
   scruffy: dirty and untidy
   casual: informal

   Which ones would you use to describe the people you have just been listening to? Why?

2  Do you agree that we tend to judge people by their appearance? Should we?

### Improve your wordpower

1  These adjectives can all be used to describe someone's character and personality.

| | | |
|---|---|---|
| shy | tense | polite |
| assertive | nervous | mean |
| aggressive | rude | kind |
| frank | loyal | reliable |
| generous | sensitive | patient |
| easy-going | stubborn | ambitious |
| sensible | trustworthy | selfish |

   Match the words to these definitions. If necessary, use a dictionary.

*a*  _____ = having deep understanding and awareness. It is often confused with *sensible* which is having the ability to make good decisions based on reasons rather than emotions.

*b*  _____ = unwilling to spend money, time, etc.; in contrast with *generous*

*c*  _____ = showing thoughts and feelings openly; honest and direct in speech

*d*  _____ = reliable and responsible; someone you can count on

*e*  _____ = remaining firm in friendship and support for someone or something

*f*  _____ = caring only about yourself

*g*  _____ = determined and unwilling to change your mind

*h*  _____ = not easily worried or upset by problems or other people's actions

2  Divide the adjectives into two lists, A and B. In A, group the adjectives which are normally used to show approval. In B, group the adjectives which normally show disapproval.

**3** Look through the list again. Find:

*a* eight adjectives that form the negative with *un-*

*b* two adjectives that form the negative with *im-*

*c* one that uses *dis-*

*d* one that uses *in-*

## Improve your writing

### Describing a person and their character

In order to provide an interesting description of a person, it is important to focus on their character and personality as well as their physical appearance. Here are some techniques. (The examples are taken from a description of a young person's brother.)

*a* Use adjectives, but provide examples that support your statements. For examples, we can describe the way they talk and relate to family, friends, strangers, etc.

*In the company of our parents he is evasive and shy about his attitudes to girls. When dad teases him about them his nose and cheeks turn bright red. At home Alan says very little, but as soon as he meets up with friends he changes. He becomes so talkative that his friends often tell him to shut up.*

*b* We can link character to dress and appearance.

*Alan usually wears a dark blue jacket. He thinks it makes him look more mature, and it suits him.*

*c* Relate character to mannerisms and normal behaviour.

*Alan is normally quite easy-going, but he does worry about his appearance and his hair! He spends a lot of time in the bathroom trying to flatten it with water.*

*d* Finally, we can also link character to physical appearance.

*Alan is short and well-built, which makes him look quite tough, but he is in fact a quiet, sensitive person.*

## PRACTICE

**1** Read this description and insert an appropriate adjective into each gap.

My aunt is one of my favourite people. She has always been very _____ (*a*). I can remember that she once spent days reading to me when I was ill. She is also very _____ (*b*) and always remembers to send me a present on my birthday, but the main reason why I like her is that she is so much more _____ (*c*) than my dad. He's always getting at me because of my _____ (*d*) black hair and _____ (*e*) clothes but she has never disapproved, and is quite _____ (*f*) to take me as I am. I like that.

Write a similar piece about a family member you like or dislike.

**2** Put the words into the correct order.

*a* My uncle has short/hair/blonde.

*b* Alan has large/eyes/brown.

*c* Karen has dark/pretty/long/eyelashes.

*d* Peter has a scruffy/leather/jacket/brown.

*e* He has a accent/Irish/lovely/soft.

*f* Helen wore a stunning/dress/red/silk.

**3** Complete these sentences about your own behaviour and mannerisms.

*a* When I feel shy I _____.

*b* When I am impatient I often _____.

*c* When I am nervous I usually _____.

*d* When my parents ask me what I have been doing I usually _____.

## WRITING

Use the *Improve your writing* notes to write a description of yourself for a class magazine. Do it from the point of view of someone that knows you well, like a close friend or a member of your family. The description should reflect the different sides you present to the world, e.g. the way you speak to different people, the way you dress in different situations, etc. Do not use the first person (*I*) in your piece of writing. Write about 140 words.

# Over to You!

## GAMES PEOPLE PLAY

### WARM-UP

1 Match the names of the games to the pictures.

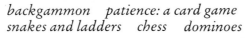

*backgammon    patience: a card game*
*snakes and ladders    chess    dominoes*

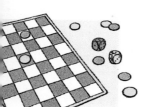

2 Which of these games requires *a board*, *dice*, or *counters*?

3 Have you played any of these games? Which ones?

4 What are the most popular games in your country? What do you think of them?

### TALKING POINT
### MONOPOLY

Monopoly is a board game. It was invented in Britain in 1935. Since then more than fifty million sets have been sold throughout the world. It is still one of the most popular games.

Monopoly is a game of chance and skill in which the players try to buy land and buildings, charge rent for them, build new property on the land, etc. They win the game by making the other players lose all their money so that the winner owns everything.

Monopoly has some of the elements of a 'trail game'. In a trail game the object is to reach the end of the game before the other players. The dice, the layout of the board, the cards, etc. are all used to provide an element of chance.

1 Have any of you ever played Monopoly? Did you like it? Why/Why not? Can you explain why it has been so popular?

2 Do you think games like Monopoly can be harmful? Why/Why not?

**Research**

*Aim:*

I) to design and produce a trail game which can be played by the other members of your class.

### *Hot tips!*

- Choose a topic area for your game, e.g. 'Getting through a school year'.
- List the events that help or slow down your progress. (You do not need to be entirely serious!)
- Set these out on a large piece of paper. As you do this think carefully about the number of squares a player will move forwards or backwards as a result of a particular event.
- If possible, add some chance cards as well (e.g. You break a leg. Back two.).

# STREETWISE
## ISSUE 8

## A FRIEND IN NEED...

## A NATIONAL GAME

## MUSIC POWER

# A FRIEND IN NEED...

## WARM-UP

Read the introductory text and discuss the answers to the questions in a small group.

There have been a series of thefts of property and money in your school, and various things seem to have disappeared. Nobody has owned up, so the police have been called in. They are looking into the problem, but so far nobody has been arrested for the crime.

One day you call in on your best friend. He is out, and his mother asks you to wait in his room. As you wait for him to turn up you start looking round, and decide to have a look at some of his books. You come across a Discman which was taken from school a week ago. You go hot and cold.

You don't want to lose a friend. You don't want to break up his family – he already has enough trouble with his dad. On the other hand, theft is a serious crime, and the police are involved. If you turn a blind eye, you'll be letting your other schoolfriends down. If you tell the police, you'll be drawn in.

What do you do? Do you turn your friend in?

*Glossary*

**Discman:** portable compact disc player made by the company that first developed the Walkman

| Grammar quiz |
| --- |

### Phrasal verbs

1   A phrasal verb is a verb + preposition/abverb particle combination. The combination usually has a different meaning from the words used separately.

Which of these examples is a phrasal verb?

*When he looked into the room he saw nobody.*
*The police looked into the case.*

2   Read the passage and find all the phrasal verbs. When you find them write them down in the infinitive form, e.g. *to call someone in.*

3   Match 7 of the verbs you have found to these definitions.

   *a*   to visit (on the way to somewhere else)
   *b*   to fail to help someone
   *c*   to become involved (in something)
   *d*   to take someone to the police
   *e*   to admit to a crime
   *f*   to arrive (often unexpectedly)
   *g*   to investigate and examine the facts

## PRACTICE

1   Complete these sentences with a suitable phrasal verb.

*a*   He was late. He didn't _____ until ten o'clock.
*b*   'Have you found the letter?' 'Yes, I was lucky. I _____ it yesterday.'
*c*   The family _____ when they left the island.
*d*   I _____ my grandad on my way home.
*e*   My best friend never _____ me _____ . He is always there when I need him.
*f*   I _____ ways of getting to America cheaply but there were no flights on the dates I wanted.

## PRONUNCIATION 😐

### Sentence stress

The verb and the preposition/particle in phrasal verbs are usually stressed. Pronouns between the verb and the preposition/particle are not stressed.

1   Decide how you would read these pairs of sentences.

*a*   *He broke up his family.*
      *He broke them up.*
*b*   *He called the police in.*
      *He called them in.*
*c*   *He turned in his friend.*
      *He turned him in.*

2   Listen and repeat.

## TALKING POINT

The situation in the *Warm-up* exercise was adapted from an advertisement aimed at getting young people to join the police force. It explores the dilemma young police officers may have when they discover their friends are breaking the law. But do some jobs put more stress on friendships and relationships than others?

Work in a small group and decide which of these jobs puts the greatest stress on friendships and relationships.

police officer     pop star
nurse on shift work     tax inspector
laboratory scientist

Be ready to state your decision and the reasons for it.

## Improve your wordpower

Match these phrasal verbs to their definitions.

get on with    put up with    stick up for
let (someone) down    get over
break down    break up    count on
look up to

*a*  support or defend someone, oneself, etc.
*b*  end a relationship (with someone)
*c*  have a friendly relationship with someone
*d*  rely on someone to help and support you
*e*  respect and admire someone.
*f*  tolerate or accept a situation that is unsatisfactory
*g*  recover from an unhappy experience, e.g. a broken relationship, illness, etc.
*h*  lose control of your emotions
*i*  disappoint someone, usually by failing to help/not doing something you promised

## PRACTICE

1  Use the phrasal verbs you have just been studying to tell Greta's story.

You're wonderful!

I still love you . . .

ODEON CINEMA
He said he would be here.

I'm so much happier!

Example
*I used to go out with a man named Michael. I looked up to him and thought he was wonderful . . .*

---

2  Substitute the verbs in **bold** with a suitable phrasal verb.

*a*  She really **respects and admires** her best friend.
*b*  They have decided to **investigate** computer dating.
*c*  They **ended their relationship** when they went to university.
*d*  He has **recovered from** his illness.
*e*  I **tolerated** her bad manners because I loved her.

### Glossary

**chaff and grain:** wheat

grain    chaff

*To separate the wheat from the chaff* is an idiom meaning to distinguish what is valuable from what is worthless.

## READING 🙁

Read this poem about friendship and answer the questions.

*Friendship*

Oh, the comfort, the inexpressible comfort,
Of feeling safe with a person,
Having neither to weigh thoughts, nor measure words,
But pour them all out, just as they are,
Chaff and grain together,
Knowing that a faithful hand will take them and sift them,
Keep what is worth keeping,
And then, with the breath of kindness,
Blow the rest away.

George Eliot (1819–80)

1  Which of these sentences is the best summary of the ideas in *Friendship*?

*a*  You feel safe with a good friend because they never say anything that hurts you.
*b*  You need to think carefully about what you say to a good friend.
*c*  Being with a good friend is a comfort because you can say what you want.
*d*  Good friends never worry about anything that you say to them.

2  What do you think of the ideas in *Friendship*?

3  Work individually and complete the sentence *A good friend is . . .*

Example
A good friend *is someone who you can count on and who will always be there when you need them.*

Read your sentence to the class. Do you all agree? What do *you* expect from a good friend?

# MUSIC POWER

## WARM-UP

Listen to the tape and follow the instructions.

Now talk about your experience in a small group.

*a* What was the effect of the music on tape?

*b* What kind of music did you 'hear' in the warm-up exercise, if any? Is it the type of music you usually listen to or not?

## READING

Before you read the text, look at these statements and decide if they are true or false.

*a* There are few places where we can avoid hearing music.

*b* Our taste in music is personal.

*c* Music can affect us physically.

*d* The only music which affects us positively is music that we like.

*e* Music can be used to cure people in hospitals.

*f* Certain types of music can be harmful.

Now read the text and see if the passage supports your answers.

### THE POWER OF MUSIC

Nowadays it's almost impossible to escape from music, even if we want to. It thunders out of every high-street shop, hisses horribly through other people's stereos on public transport, lulls you in hotel lobbies and restaurants, and blasts out of wound-down car and van windows.

But, although we all can now have music wherever we go, very few of us have any real idea of the effect music has on the human system. For many years it has been assumed that musical tastes are subjective – that one person will like jazz while another prefers classical.

But recent research in America and Australia has shown that appreciation of music is not a matter of individual taste. Certain types of music will have a particular effect on us, regardless of whether we 'like' them or not. For instance, some music will help us feel relaxed and peaceful, whereas other types may be stimulating to the brain, encouraging curiosity and alertness. Some music promotes loving feelings; other sounds whip up hate, jealousy, and violence.

As a result, music is being used in hospitals,

*Glossary*

**lull:** cause you to feel calm

and doctors have found that 20 minutes of soothing music is often far more effective than tranquillisers or sleeping pills. For example, after a recent operation, Fiona Richmond, 15, was not allowed to listen to her favourite heavy metal group. Instead, she was made to listen to baroque music because it was good for her.

According to researcher Susan Burghardt, all music can be divided into three types, and each one has profound effects on the body and mind. The first is low-energy music, the sort that makes you feel bad. Most rock music falls into this category. In fact it has been discovered that rock music makes people feel hate instead of love. The work of some classical composers, such as Debussy and Schoenberg, has also been found to be harmful.

The next category is high-energy music. This makes you feel better and it can help to normalize heart rate. J S Bach is exceptionally high energy.

The third category is prayerful music. This is the most healing of all. Much of the classical music written before 1600 falls into this category.

It seems that most Jazz and Country and Western is simply neutral, having neither a healing nor harming effect.

Scientific work on the healing power of music started with plant research in the 1970s. Many types of classical music speeded plant growth, whereas heavy metal caused plants to draw away from the speakers and die.

Answer the questions.

1 Does music affect our bodies in the same way? If necessary, revise your answers to the pre-reading task.

2 Does all music harm or heal?

3 Complete this table.

| Type of music | Example | Effect |
|---|---|---|
| low-energy | | |

4 Do you believe that rock music can be harmful? Why/Why not?

## VOCABULARY

1 What is the meaning of these words from the text?

*a* thunder out    *e* whip up

*b* hiss    *f* soothing

*c* blast out    *g* profound

*d* subjective    *h* speakers

2 Check your answers with your partner before consulting a dictionary and/or your teacher.

## Improve your grammar

### make, let, and allowed to

Active: *He made her listen to Beethoven when she was younger.*
Passive: *She was made to listen to Beethoven when she was younger.*
Active: *The doctors did not let her listen to loud music.*
Passive: *She was not allowed to listen to loud music.*
(NOT *She wasn't let to listen...*)

1 If we make someone do something, we force them to do it. If we want to use *make* in the passive in this sense we must add *to*.
2 We cannot use *let* in the passive. Instead, we have to use *allowed to*.

## PRACTICE 1

1 Complete these sentences with an appropriate form of *make*, *let* or *allow*.

a When I was a boy my father ____ me listen to classical music. I hated it.
b ____ you ____ to go out alone at night when you were younger?
c His father usually ____ him listen to pop music while he does his homework. My father doesn't ____ me.
d My mother used to ____ me go to bed at nine o'clock.
e He wants to go. Why don't you ____ him?
f I was ____ to eat carrots. I still dislike them.

2 Make as many sentences as you can about these situations using *make*, *let* and *allow*.

a Fiona did not want to listen to classical music but the doctors insisted.
b Alan wanted to play in a rock band but his father told him he couldn't.
c Alice wanted to go to the disco but her mother told her she had to finish her homework first.
d Chris did not like piano lessons but his parents told him to go.
e His teachers gave him permission to play the electric guitar in music lessons.
f Sandra has to wear headphones to listen to heavy metal.

3 Tell a partner some of the things your parents or teachers made you do or didn't let you do when you were younger.

Dad! Is it alright if I listen to my music?

## Improve your wordpower

The following adjectives are often used to describe music. Make sure you know the meaning of each one.

soothing    traditional    discordant    loud
violent      joyful         romantic      harsh
gentle       rhythmic       melodious     sad

Now listen to four extracts of music. How would you describe each one?

## GETTING STREETWISE!
### Permission

When we need to ask permission, the words we choose will depend on who we are speaking to, the amount of resistance we expect, etc.

Look at each of these situations. How polite would you have to be? What would you say?

a You are visiting friends with your parents. An important basketball match is on television. You want to watch it.
b You are staying with friends. You want to phone your parents who are in New York.
c You are by the pool with a friend. You want to use their sun cream.

Now listen to some possible responses.

a What expressions were used to ask permission? Which of these was the most formal? Which was the most informal?
b What expressions did the speakers use to give permission?
c What was used to refuse permission?

## PRACTICE 2

Work in pairs and build conversations.

a You want your teacher's permission to have a disco in school.
b You want your parents' permission to buy a new stereo.

Each conversation should follow this pattern:

**Student A**                    **Student B**

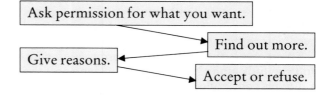

# A NATIONAL GAME

## WARM-UP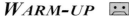

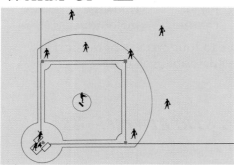

Baseball is the USA's national game. Look at the pictures here and on the cover and discuss what you know about the game.

Now listen to a description of the game and label the diagram with words from this list.

pitcher   home base   first base   umpire
batter   fielder   catcher

## READING

### A BASEBALL GAME

Every aspect of a professional baseball game is enormous fun. For example, the fans – they just love eating. After two or three innings (each side plays nine) the stands begin to empty. This is in spite of the fact that throughout the game vendors walk around calling 'Get your hot dogs, they're red-hot!', or 'Never fear, I got ice-cold beer!' These limited choices are not enough. To get the full range of food, you have to go behind the seats to a vast covered market of fast food.

There are hot dogs and burgers, and sandwiches and pizza and chilli, and candy and popcorn, and every kind of soda. There are also regional specialties.

By the fourth or fifth innings, halfway through the game, the queues at the stands snake round the stadium's gangways. At most places you need to stand in a separate line for each different item, so you could spend the best part of the game merely refuelling yourself and your party. Luckily each concession has its own closed-circuit TV, so you don't actually miss the game. Indeed you have all the comforts of home without ever leaving the stadium.

The result is that when you return to your seat, you can look along the row of fellow fans and see a magnificent collection of bellies. Bare bellies, bellies in T-shirts, bellies with yet more food

*Glossary*

**mitt:** a special glove worn by the fielders in baseball

**major league:** the most important professional teams play in the major league

**home team:** the team which normally plays in that stadium and therefore the team that most of the spectators will support

**Yo:** Hey you! (an informal way of getting attention)

**rituals:** procedures that people follow regularly, the same way each time

balanced upon them. Now and again a belly will quiver as its owner, seeing a vendor, cries 'Hey, beer!' or 'Yo! Hot dog!' If you walk down the crowded row of a theatre, people move their feet and legs. Here they take a deep breath.

I love the rituals of each game. I like the way the organ always plays 'Take Me Out to the Ball Game'. I like the 'Seventh Inning Stretch' when the fans do exercises before their team bats for the seventh time. When the ball is hit into the stands, whoever catches it can keep it, so small boys bring their mitts from home. They have little chance of catching a ball, but if they did, it would have magical powers, having once been hit by a major league player. When a spectator makes a good catch, the public announcer will almost always say, 'Give that fan a contract!'

These small rituals must have a soothing effect. Certainly a baseball crowd always seems cheerful, even when the home team has lost. Maybe they are all full of too much food to care.

1  Why do the stands begin to empty shortly after the start of the game?
2  What did the writer mean by these statements?
*a*  Indeed you have all the comforts of home without ever leaving the stadium.
*b*  If you walk down the crowded row of a theatre, people move their feet and legs. Here they take a deep breath.

## VOCABULARY

1  Match the words and definitions.

*a*  vendors            stomach
*b*  range              shake and tremble
*c*  gangways           set of products
*d*  belly              passage between
                        rows of seats in a
                        stadium
*e*  quiver             people who sell
                        from a stall or cart

## TALKING POINT

Work in pairs or small groups.

1  List the similarities and differences between a professional baseball game and another professional sports event you have been to or seen on television. Think about:

the nature of the game – team or individual
the atmosphere in the stadium
the mood of the spectators
the rituals

2  Read your list to the class and see if they agree or disagree.

## Improve your writing

### Describing an event

*a* Decide on the purpose of the description before you begin. Do you want to give information or entertain? If you want to give information, make sure that you give a clear step-by-step account.

   If you want to entertain, make sure that you include details about the atmosphere of the event, the mood of the participants (what did they wear/do/etc?), the rituals, etc.

*b* What does your audience know? Will you need to explain any technical terms or non-English words?

*c* Decide on your tenses. If you are writing about a *specific* event that you attended, then use the past tense. Otherwise, present tenses are more appropriate.

*d* It is important to describe what happens in sequence. These expressions can help:

   *the day before/after*
   *in the morning/afternoon/evening*
   *at the start/end of the day*
   *as soon as/when/after/before*

## PRACTICE

Complete this text with appropriate expressions from the box. Note that there are more expressions than you need.

> the night before   a few hours before   before
> after   the start of   a few minutes before
> at the end of   until   when
> a few minutes after

**The FA (Football Association) Cup final**

The English FA Cup final is played in Wembley stadium in North London. Most teams spend _____ (*a*) the game in hotels near the ground. _____ (*b*) kick-off, they take the short bus journey to the stadium. The players like to walk on the pitch and sample the atmosphere _____ (*c*) they change into their football kit. As _____ (*d*) the game approaches the crowd gets noisier and nosier. The crowd usually does a lot of singing. Members of the royal family usually attend and _____ (*e*) the

game starts, they are introduced to both teams. The teams then get a chance for a little practice _____ (*f*) it is time for the referee to start the game.

## Use and usage

### Group nouns

A group noun refers to a group of people. It can take a singular or a plural verb. The choice depends on whether we see the group as a whole:

*His family is very interesting.*
*The orchestra has some new players.*

or as a number of individuals:

*His family are very kind.*
*The orchestra don't seem to be playing very well.*

In American English, group nouns are always singular.

Some common group nouns are:

*group, crowd, team, audience, orchestra, choir.*

Use one of the group nouns and *is* or *are* in these sentences.

*a* The orchestra is ready, the _____ waiting. The concert is about to start.

*b* The _____ practising with an orchestra for the first time.

*c* The _____ going crazy. Their team has won.

## WRITING

Use the *Improve your writing* guidelines to write a description of an important national occasion – for example a cup final, a festival or another event. You should assume you are writing for someone from another culture. Your objective is to inform and entertain.

# ADVERTISING

## READING

### THE POWER OF ADVERTISING

Advertising often uses language and pictures to make us believe that we should be ashamed of ourselves for not buying a certain product for ourselves or our families. They play on our feelings, emotions, and especially our wish to:

1  Be up-to-date and knowledgeable.
   Advertisers expect us to believe what 'the experts' say about their products. We find expressions like 'a revolution in skin care' or 'scientifically developed'.

2  Be as good as others.
   They challenge us to 'keep up-to-date', 'keep up with the neighbours', or even 'keep one jump ahead'. The message is to buy the product if we don't want to be left behind.

3  Be attractive.
   Pictures of attractive people are used to draw attention to a product, and the suggestion is that we will be desirable and socially successful if we use that product.

4  Do things well.
   The idea is that you must buy the product if you want to do your job properly. Many soap powders are sold through the idea that they 'wash whiter than white', 'remove stains', etc.

5  Be responsible or act responsibly.
   Adverts for health foods, environmentally-friendly products, and even charities, appeal to the caring side of human nature. They aim to make us feel guilty if we ignore the appeal.

6  Have excitement in our lives.
   Pictures of exciting or romantic events are used to suggest that exciting things happen when we use a particular product.

7  Be one of the group ... or an individual.
   Some people like knowing that lots of people have chosen the same product, so expressions like 'millions of satisfied users' are used to reassure them. Sometimes advertisers try to convey the idea that only 'special' people use their product. They will use expressions like ' a unique experience'.

8  Be shrewd and streetwise.
   We sometimes feel guilty about spending money. Advertisers reassure us and suggest that we are making a good decision by offering us 'great value', 'mammoth savings', and 'bargains of the century', etc.

1  Examine these examples of advertiser's language. What is each advertisement suggesting to the consumer?

## TALKING POINT

1  Which feelings would you play on to sell these products?

   washing-up liquid     designer jeans
   glucose 'sports' drink

   Which of these adjectives would be most suitable. Why?

   | best | safe | gentle |
   | free | economical | new |
   | luxury | cheap | soft |
   | super | strong | sparkling |
   | healthy | long-lasting | refreshing |

2  Produce an advertisement for one of the products.

### Research

*Aim:*

1)  to analyse and present examples of adverts to show which feelings they appeal to. Pay special attention to the combination of language and illustrations.

Save! Save!

A real bargain!

Guaranteed to ...

The latest

New!

Best ever!

Special!

A once-in-a-lifetime chance!

Can you afford to miss this opportunity?

Sale of the century

Bargains galore!

You can help

# GRAMMAR REVIEW ISSUES 7 AND 8

## SEQUENCE OF ADJECTIVES

When we use more than one adjective with a noun we have to take care with the word order. There are no absolute rules, since a lot depends on the emphasis a speaker wishes to make. Here is a general guide:

| opinion | size/age/ shape | colour | origin | material | noun |
|---|---|---|---|---|---|
| beautiful stunning | large new square | red gold | Japanese | velvet | kimono chairs |

1. General qualities come before particular ones.
   *creamy white sponge cake*
2. Personal opinions go before more objective words.
   *beautiful tall building*
3. Size generally precedes age and shape, etc.
   *a big old house*
   *a small round table*

### Notes

Adjectival past participles are usually closest to the noun.
*a handmade sweater*
*an outdated telephone book*
*an elevated railway*

We usually use a maximum of two or three adjectives before the noun, adding extra details afterwards.
*gold plated telephone cards, personalized with the guest's name*

## TOO AND ENOUGH

1. *too* goes before adjectives and adverbs, and conveys the idea of 'more than is necessary' or 'excess'. Do not confuse this with the intensifier *very* which does not have the idea of 'excess'.

   *It looked too beautiful to be real.*
   *My father works too hard.*
   *The bride was very beautiful.* (NOT ... too beautiful)

2. *enough* can come after adjectives and adverbs. It means that the person can or can't do the thing that is mentioned because of their age, speed, etc.

   *She is old enough to marry.*
   *I wasn't fast enough to catch up with them.*

It can also come before nouns to express the idea of 'as much as you need'.

*They do not have enough time to do the exercise.*
*I've had enough cake, thank you.*

## COMPARATIVES AND MODIFIERS

Words like *very*, *too* and *quite* can modify adjectives, e.g. *very tall*, *too young*, *quite old*, but not comparatives.

*He's very old.* (NOT *He's very older*.)

To modify comparisons we use expressions like *much*, *far*, *a lot*, *lots*, *rather*, *hardly any*, *a little*, *a bit*, etc.

*It's much/ a little/ a bit colder than yesterday.*
*Prices are much/ a little higher in New York.*
*He is hardly any/ a little bit taller than his brother.*

Expressions like *considerably*, *marginally*, *slightly* provide for degrees of comparison.

*The pass rate in mixed schools is considerably lower.*

We can also use *no* + comparative to emphasise similarity or to show there has been no change.

*Peter is a terrible tennis player, and his brother is no better.*
*'Is your uncle still in hospital?' 'Yes, I'm afraid he's no better.'*

## PHRASAL VERBS
### Form

verb + preposition/adverb particle (e.g. *down, up, out, after*, etc.)

Some phrasal verbs require an object (i.e. are 'transitive').

| | verb | object | preposition/adverb particle |
|---|---|---|---|
| I | picked | the letter | up. |
| He | let | his brother | down. |

Others cannot take an object (i.e. are 'intransitive').

| | verb | preposition/adverb particle |
|---|---|---|
| Their marriage | broke | down. |
| The plane | took | off. |

### Meaning

1. In some cases the meaning of the phrasal verb is clear from the verb + preposition/adverb particle combination.

   *He put the picture up on the outside wall.*
2. Sometimes the combination has a special meaning.
   *He puts up with a lot.* (= tolerates or accepts an unpleasant situation)

## Word order

1 When the verb takes an object, the preposition/ adverb particle can come:
a before the object, e.g. *He picked up the letter.*
b after the object, e.g. *He picked the letter up.*
2 If the object is very long, it comes after the particle.

*He picked up the letter and the envelopes that were with it.*

3 If the object is a pronoun (e.g. *them, it,* etc.) it usually comes before the particle.

*He picked them up.* (NOT He picked up them.)

However, some phrasal verbs take an object but we do not separate them from the particle.

*My uncle looked after me as a child.* (NOT ... looked me after ...)

## MAKE, LET, ALLOW
### Make

1 If we make someone or something do something, we force them to do it. We need an object.
2 *make* in the active is followed by base form without *to.*

*He made her listen to Beethoven when she was younger.*
*He made me move my car.*

3 *make* in the passive is followed by base form with *to.*
*She was made to listen to Beethoven when she was younger*
*I was made to move my car.*

### Let and allow

1 If you let or allow someone to do something, especially someone you have authority over, you give them permission or do not try to stop them.

*After thinking about it, my father let me take driving lessons.*
*I was allowed to go provided I was home by 11.*

2 *Let* is followed by base form without *to* in the active. *Let* does not have a passive form and is replaced by *allowed to.*
Active: My parents let me go to the disco.
Passive: I was allowed to go to the disco.
(NOT I was let go to the disco.)

# GRAMMAR PRACTICE

## A

1 Complete the sentences with an appropriate comparative or superlative form of the adjectives in brackets. Make any additions you need.

Examples
I am *younger than* my sister. (young)
He isn't as *old as* he looks. (old)
They are the *best* in the class. (good)

a Which is the _____ city in your country? (large)
b His writing is as _____ mine. (bad)
c Who is the _____ student in class? (serious)
d The bride was as _____ he was. (tall)
e She is one of the _____ people I know. (attractive)
f The cakes were as _____ the sandwiches. (good)
g He was _____ his brother. (short)
h He has the _____ house from the school. (far)

2 Complete the sentences with *too* or *enough* and an adjective from the box.

> hot   sweet   old   fast   late   loud   expensive

a I can't drink this! It's _____ .
b He's only fifteen. He isn't _____ to drive.
c He hasn't won any races this year. His car isn't _____ .
d I didn't have enough money to buy it. It was _____ .
e 'We can't hear the TV.' 'Sorry. Isn't it _____ ?'
f I'm afraid we were _____ to catch the plane.
g Could I have some more sugar please? It's not _____ .

3 Put *to* into the blanks only if it's necessary.
a I allowed him _____ go.
b She let her daughter _____ stay out till midnight.
c He made him _____ stand outside for the whole lesson.
d I wasn't allowed _____ watch the programme on TV.
e Did she let you _____ borrow her cassettes?
f He always makes me _____ wait for him.
g She was made _____ wear those shoes.
h My mum never lets me _____ go to films alone.
i The film was very funny. It made me _____ laugh.
j My older brother used to make me _____ cry.

## B

**1** Rewrite these sentences so that they keep the same meaning.

*a* She isn't old enough to vote.
She is too _____ .

*b* I didn't have enough time to finish.
I had too _____ .

*c* She was too young to go in.
She wasn't _____ .

*d* He's rich enough to own a plane.
He's not too _____ .

*e* The weather was too cold to swim.
The weather wasn't _____ .

**2** Decide on the best word-order.
Example
tiny Japanese computer new a
*a tiny new Japanese computer*

*a* short hair brown horrible

*b* plastic shoes cheap

*c* middle-aged a man handsome

*d* cakes small round three

*e* beautiful dress blue a

*f* tie attractive an old handpainted

*g* young an woman Irish intelligent

**3** Complete the following sentences with one word.
Example
Look! There's something on the floor. Pick it *up*!

*a* The music is too soft. Turn it _____ .

*b* Why don't you give _____ smoking? It's bad for you.

*c* He was walking in the street when he came _____ ten dollars.

*d* The police said they would look _____ the thefts.

*e* I'm looking _____ my lost keys.

*f* Who looked _____ you as a child?

*g* My sister doesn't see him any more. They broke _____ two weeks ago.

**4** Replace the words in italics with a pronoun.
Example
Do you get on with *the Smiths*?
*Do you get on with them?*

*a* He let *his friends* down.

*b* I called in on *my aunt* on the way home.

*c* I don't want to put up with *Sally's* rudeness any more.

*d* They put *the building* up in less than a week.

*e* He hasn't got over *the match* yet.

**5** Use *make*, *let* and *allow* to write a sentence for each of these situations.
Example
Sara wanted to go to a pop concert. Here father said she couldn't go because she hadn't finished her homework.
*He made her stay at home.*
*He didn't let her go to the concert.*
*She wasn't allowed to go.*

*a* The teacher told the class that they had to stay behind until they had all finished the exercise.

*b* Alice wanted to go to the cinema but her mother told her to stay at home and help her with the housework.

*c* Alice's brother is doing military service. He had long hair before, but it is now very short.

*d* Tom was very tired after doing thirty lengths of the swimming pool, but his coach told him to do ten more.

## C

**1** A pen friend is thinking of buying her brother either a dog or a cat as a pet. She has asked your opinion on which is better. Use the words below as part of your answer.

intelligent  well-behaved  gentle  obedient  a lot
independent  clean  aggressive  a little  much

**2** Use all the words below to describe the furniture in the pictures.

modern  old  Chinese  table  uncomfortable
office  chair  desk  wooden  valuable  attractive

**3** You are writing to a pen friend. Use *make*, *let* and *allow* to write a short paragraph describing how the adults in your house treat you.

# Wise up!

## LISTENING

### FACTORS IN LISTENING COMPREHENSION

Suppose we start listening to two people at the next table in a restaurant or café. Our ability to follow and understand them will depend on factors such as:

- our knowledge of the language.
- background knowledge.
  *How much do we know about what they are talking about?*
- knowledge of the situation.
  *Who are they? What is their relationship? etc.*
- how much we already know of what has been said.

In addition there will also be external factors such as the amount of noise, whether we can see their faces, etc., although these can be overcome to some extent by our ability to predict what they will say.

In short, to listen effectively we need to activate as much knowledge as we can.

*1* In some situations, such as hiring a car or buying an ice-cream, people are sometimes able to follow quite a lot of a foreign language they do not speak. Why is this so? What are the implications for your listening in English?

### BECOMING A BETTER LISTENER

The best way of improving is to get as much practice in listening as possible. Some of this may be 'real' English on television and radio. You may find authentic listening quite difficult at first, but try your best and it will become easier.

- Use your knowledge of the world to help you predict or guess what people are talking about.
- Never stop listening too early. Quite a lot of what is said may be repeated.
- Do not worry if you cannot understand every word. We rarely follow everything we hear, even in our own language.

*1* Where can you listen to English outside class? What are some of the things you can listen to?

### WHAT THE EXAMINER WANTS

Listening exams employ a variety of techniques. These may include:

- answering true or false questions.
- sentence completion.
- ticking the right boxes.
- extracting essential information, e.g. train times, from a longer message.
- information transfer, e.g. completing a diagram using information on tape.
- matching a picture to what you hear on tape.

*1* Find out how any exam you are going to take tests listening comprehension.

### IMPROVING EXAM PERFORMANCE

Most listening exams allow candidates time to look through the questions before the listening begins. Use this time to look through the questions so that you:

- know what you are required to do.
- can use the context to help you predict the content of the listening, as this will help you activate what you know.

*1* Look at these examples of exam questions.

a | *Put a tick (✓) against the two young people Ken Brown describes.*

Make a quick list of the words you expect to hear.

b | *Fill in the missing information in the messages Anthea wrote for her father.*
Mr Jones (tel. no. _____) (1) wants you to paint _____ . (2)

Mrs Jones rang.
She was very _____ . (3)
Can you go and see why her new wall _____ ? (4)

List the words you might expect to use in the blanks.

c | *Put a tick in the box that corresponds to the woman's answers.*
**Does she usually go to Spain for her holidays?**
Yes ☐
No ☐
Where did she go last year? ☐

What do you expect to hear?

# STREETWISE
## ISSUE 9

## WORTH A THOUSAND WORDS?

## IF ONLY...

What price a cycle helmet?

## OVER-TRAINED AND UNDER STRESS?

# WORTH A THOUSAND WORDS?

## *WARM-UP*

Discuss these questions in small groups.

People say a good picture is worth a thousand words. Why? Is this true? How much do pictures contribute to newspaper and magazine stories? Are there any pictures you would rather not see?

## *READING* ☹

Bob Geldof is a pop singer. He is, however, best known as the organiser of Band Aid, a series of concerts and events to raise money to help starving people in Ethiopia. In this extract from his life story *Is That it?* Geldof argues with a well-known photographer.

### PUBLISH AND BE DAMNED?

'You really do have to understand this. I do not want any pictures of me with starving children. We've seen them before, visiting politicians looking fat and concerned as they hold a child in their arms who is near to the point of death from malnutrition, who may well die the day after the western celebrities and their photographers have left the camp.'

'Bob, you know that's the picture we've been sent to get, you with one of the children who Band Aid is trying to help. That is the picture,' said Kenny Lennox of the *Daily Star*.

'I know it is. And that is the picture I don't want. It's disgustingly sensational. It degrades the people involved. It's exploiting their misery to give you a nice shot.'

I did not trust them. Earlier Kenny had told me that he was one of the photographers who had taken photographs of Princess Diana in her bikini when she was pregnant. In all other respects he was a nice bloke. He spoke of his own child in relation to the kids that we saw in a way that was sensitive and moving. But it was weird, as soon as he started to do his job he seemed to throw all sense of personal morality on one side. He told me how he had lain out in a boat for a couple of nights to get that bikini picture. He was clearly proud of himself.

'The public have the right to know,' he parroted.

'Right to know what?' I asked. 'Why do you want to hurt people? Did you take pictures of your own wife when she was pregnant and show everyone in the neighbourhood? Is the woman not allowed to enjoy her pregnancy in private? I don't suppose she went to the beach in her bikini again after that!'

In trying to defend himself he revealed that he had been one of the photographers who had prevented Elizabeth Taylor from going to mourn alone at Richard Burton's grave. Sometimes, he said, one photographer would be prepared to make concessions but was unable to do so because a competitor would refuse to do the same. She had risen before dawn to be at the grave before anybody else was up. When Liz got to the cemetery gates she had been confronted by photographers and had pleaded with them to leave her alone, just that once.

'We said we were all going to leave, and then one guy said he wouldn't go. What could we do? We couldn't leave him to be the only one who got the picture. What would our editors say?'

'So what happened?'

'Well, as it happened there weren't any pictures, because when we wouldn't go she didn't go in. She just went away.'

'So she didn't get the chance to say her last goodbye. Are you proud of that?'

'No, but if I'd gone, the other bloke would have taken the picture. So it would have happened whatever I did.'

'So because this woman is a star she has no right to mourn privately? Is that it, Kenny? That's unacceptable.'

I went to each photographer and made each swear on his honour not to do it. They all did, even Kenny.

### Glossary

**The Daily Star:** a tabloid newspaper with sensational stories (often about the private lives of the famous)

**parroted:** repeated without thinking or understanding

**Elizabeth Taylor:** famous American film star. She has been married eight times, twice to the actor Richard Burton who died in 1984.

*1* Complete this table:

| Photo | Reasons why Kenny wanted the picture | Bob's arguments against | Your opinion |
|---|---|---|---|
| Geldof and the children | | | |
| Princess Diana in her bikini when pregnant | | | |
| Elizabeth Taylor grieving at her husband's grave | | | |

2 What is the unstated reason for wanting the pictures?

3 Which is the best summary of Bob's view of Kenny? Why?

a He thinks Kenny is a nice man who loves children.

b He doesn't like Kenny and thinks he is totally immoral.

c He thinks Kenny is nice except when he is working.

4 '*It's* disgustingly sensational.' What is?
'I did not trust *them*.' Who does *them* refer to?
'Swear not to do *it*.' What does *it* refer to?

5 Who do you agree with more? Kenny or Bob? Why?

## VOCABULARY

1 Look back at the text. What is the meaning of the words in *italics*?

a near to the point of death from *malnutrition*
b the western *celebrities* and their photographers
c But it was *weird*
d had *pleaded with* them to leave

2 Match the words in column A to the meanings in B.

| A | B |
| --- | --- |
| degrade | use unfairly |
| trust | cause someone to lose their respect and dignity |
| exploit | agree to let someone have something to end an argument |
| mourn | believe that someone is honest and reliable |
| make concessions | show sorrow or regret over someone's death |

## PRONUNCIATION 😐

**Word stress**

Listen to the way these words are pronounced.

1 Mark the stress.

sensational
celebrity
competitor    competition
pregnant     pregnancy
photograph   photographer
politics     political      politician

2 Identify the weak form /ə/ where it occurs.
3 Listen and repeat.

*Grammar quiz*

## Third conditional

*If I had gone, the other bloke would have taken the picture.*

1 Did Kenny stay or not? How do we know?
2 Do we use this structure for events that happened or events that did not happen?

## PRACTICE

1 Put the verbs in brackets into an appropriate form using the third conditional.

a If he (not hide) in a boat, Kenny (not got) the picture of Princess Diana.

b Kenny and the others (take) a picture of Bob and the children if he (not stop) them.

c Kenny's Editor (be) very angry if he (let) the other photographer take Liz's picture.

d The tabloids (not be interested) in a picture of Liz if she (not be) a celebrity.

e If the papers (print) a picture of Bob and the starving children he (be) furious.

2 Describe what you would have done in each situation if:

a you had been Kenny.
b you had been Kenny's victim.

## LISTENING 😐

Jim Fraser is a photographer for the *Daily Telegraph*, a national newspaper. *Streetwise* went to find out more about him and his job. Listen and answer the questions.

1 What did Jim do before he worked for the *Telegraph*?
2 Why is press photography a matter of luck?
3 Why is it difficult to get good pictures of Heads of State?
4 What do you have to do to get the right picture?
5 What pictures would he regret taking?
6 Why do press photographers sometimes behave like animals?

## WRITING

Imagine you are a well-known photographer. *Streetwise* has asked you to write a description of what you had to do in order to get a secret picture of a famous criminal or celebrity.

■ Start your account by setting the background. Explain who the person is and what kind of picture you wanted.

■ Describe what you had to do to get the picture. What would have happened if you had been caught?

■ Where was the picture published? What happened as a result of its publication?

# IF ONLY...

## WARM-UP

What is the law on car seat belts and motorcycle helmets in your country?

Carry out a class survey. Find out how many students wouldn't:

a  use a seat-belt in the front of a car.
b  use a seat-belt in the back of a car.
c  wear a helmet on a motorcycle.
d  wear a helmet while riding a bicycle.

Find out why people say they would not. Do you agree with their reasons? Why/Why not?

## READING

Work in pairs. Before reading the text decide if these statements are true or false.

a  Head injury is the main cause of death in cycling accidents.
b  Bicycle helmets cut down on the risk of head injury.
c  In the UK most cyclists wear helmets.
d  Well-made helmets cost a lot.
e  Cyclists are less likely to suffer head injuries than motorcyclists.
f  A fall at low speeds can't kill.

Now check your answers by reading the text as quickly as possible.

## WHAT PRICE A CYCLE HELMET?

On a rainy November morning two years ago, Shirley Huxham was free-wheeling gently downhill. Spotting a friend, she raised a hand to wave. Shirley's bike skidded on the wet road, throwing her head first on the ground.

'I'd never even thought of buying a helmet,' she says, her speech now halting and slurred. For months partly paralysed down her left side, Shirley has impaired sight, memory and balance.

On September 2 last year, 12-year-old James Dowson was riding his new 15-speed mountain bike on a woodland track near his Sheffield home. Exhilarated, he hurtled down a steep slope and up the other side. He lost control of the bike and hit a tree. James hit his head on its trunk.

'My head took the full impact – but my injuries only started where my bike helmet stopped,' says James. His face was an appalling mess but the helmet saved his life.

Some might think that these accidents were flukes. How dangerous can it be to fall from a bicycle? And wasn't James Dowson just lucky?

In fact these incidents are typical of a national problem. Each year on Britain's roads more than 200 people are killed and at least 4,000 seriously injured on bicycles. Head injury is the main cause of death in about 70 per cent of bicycling fatalities. But these numbers don't tell the whole story: the vast majority of the dead and injured were not wearing protective helmets.

A study of bicycle accidents in the US found that helmets reduced the risk of serious head injury by 85 per cent. And yet it is estimated that less than five per cent of British cyclists wear helmets. Why don't more cyclists wear them? There are a variety of excuses: helmets look foolish; they're inconvenient; accidents happen to other people. Some mistakenly believe helmets are hot and heavy, can injure the neck or impair hearing. Others say they cost too much. Yet well-made bike helmets can be bought quite cheaply.

One of the biggest misconceptions among bicycle riders is that lower speeds put cyclists at less risk than motorcyclists, who are legally obliged to wear helmets. In fact according to a British report, a higher percentage of bicyclists than motorcyclists suffer head injuries. And their injuries can be just as severe.

Protective headgear, however, can make all the difference. James wasn't just lucky. If he hadn't worn a helmet, he would be dead and if Shirley had, she wouldn't have problems with her sight, memory, and balance. Why take the risk?

## Glossary

**free-wheeling:** travelling on a bicycle without using the pedals

**flukes:** things that happen by chance

## VOCABULARY

Find words in the text which mean:

a  slid sideways
b  unclearly or indistinctly pronounced
c  damaged
d  very happy and excited
e  travelled very fast
f  terrible
g  a wrong idea about something
h  the possibility of danger or coming to harm

## WRITING

Read the text again. This time, summarize the main ideas in the text, in five or six sentences. Use your own words as far as possible.

Start by underlining or highlighting parts of the text that provide new information.

Summarize sections that provide several examples with a key sentence e.g. *Cycling accidents can have tragic consequences including paralysis and death.*

## Improve your grammar

### Third conditional with a present outcome

Form

| *If* clause | main clause |
|---|---|
| past perfect (imagined condition) | *would* + base form (present outcome) |
| *If I had been careful,* | *I wouldn't be in hospital now.* |

We can use this form to talk about the imagined present outcome/result of an imagined past action.

Examples
*If Shirley had worn a helmet two years ago, she wouldn't have problems with her sight now.* (But she didn't wear one, so she has problems.)

*If I had had some sleep last night, I wouldn't be so tired today.* (But I didn't, so I am tired.)

## PRACTICE 1

1   Write a sentence for each situation using the third conditional with a present outcome.

Example
Simon was not wearing a helmet when he fell off his bike. He is in hospital.
*If he had been wearing a helmet, he wouldn't be in hospital now.*

*a*   James was wearing a helmet when he hit the tree. He is alive.

*b*   The government introduced a seat-belt law. My cousin now wears one.

*c*   I read an article about cycle safety. I now wear a cycle helmet.

*d*   The man who knocked a cyclist down is now in jail.

*e*   My uncle is now very rich. He started a factory which makes safety-helmets.

*f*   Shirley went skiing. She broke her leg and can't walk.

2   Complete these sentences with a present outcome.

*a*   If I hadn't started to learn English, _____ .

*b*   If I hadn't come to school today, _____ .

*c*   If we hadn't invented the motor car, _____ .

*d*   If we hadn't built all these tourist hotels, __ .

*e*   If computers had been invented in the nineteenth century, _____ .

## GETTING STREETWISE!
### Expressing regrets

Listen to extracts from four different interviews. In each case the interviewee is expressing regret about something that she or he did or didn't do.

1   Work out what each person is expressing regret about.

2   List the expressions they used to express regret.

3   Repeat the expressions following the intonation on the tape.

## Use and usage

### *wish* or *if only* + past perfect

*wish* or *if only* + past perfect refers to the past.

Examples
*I wish I had learned to play the guitar.*
*If only I had worn my seat belt.*

This structure can express regret for something that has or hasn't happened.

Complete these sentences with an appropriate verb phrase using the past perfect.

*a*   My team lost the championship in the last match. If only _____ .

*b*   I failed my exam because I was late. I wish _____ .

*c*   My friends won the lottery but I didn't join them. If only _____ .

*d*   My grandmother didn't know the table was valuable when she sold it. She wishes _____ .

## PRACTICE 2

Work in pairs and write a dialogue in which you interview someone about their past regrets. Be ready to act your dialogue out.

If only I'd used a different shampoo!

# OVER-TRAINED AND UNDER STRESS?

## *WARM-UP*

Read these extracts, and decide on the answers to these questions.

*a* What do the extracts have in common?

*b* Which extract do *you* think is the most effective? Why?

*c* What do you think of the opinions given?

### A

People used to argue that sports were of value because they built character. They claimed that games promoted hard work, sportsmanship, and the joy of playing. But to many today such arguments sound hollow, even hypocritical.

The emphasis on winning is particularly a problem. *Seventeen* magazine calls this 'a darker side of sports.' Why? Because, to quote the magazine: 'winning becomes more important than honesty, schoolwork, health, happiness and most other important aspects of life.'

### B

For many young people sport is no longer a run around a basketball court twice a week or a game of tennis on a warm day. It is a serious and expensive business involving hours of daily training. For some, that training starts at a very early age, which is reflected in the increasing number of world champions in their teens. However, recent studies suggest that overtraining can lead to stunted growth, skeletal injuries, and eating disorders in athletes who need to keep slim, such as gymnasts.

### C

Marta Neil is only nineteen. If things had worked out as planned, Marta would be playing in this week's Wimbledon championships. Instead, she will be watching the championships on television.

Marta had to give up a promising tennis career because of an injury which could have been prevented with proper rest between matches.

Marta's case illustrates the increasing concern many have about the competitiveness of modern sport and the effect this has on young people.

## *LISTENING* 😦

Karen Stevens is nineteen. She was British Junior Champion at sixteen. She has recently retired from competitive swimming.

Martin Jones is seventeen. He was a promising tennis player until he gave up last year.

*Streetwise* spoke to them to see why they gave up. Listen to the interview and note down what they saw as the positive and negative aspects of being young sports stars.

## *TALKING POINT*

Work in pairs.

*a* Use what you have heard and read to list the arguments for and against the statement. 'Sport can do more harm than good.'

*b* Take part in a debate on the topic.

---

### *Improve your writing*

#### An opinion piece

#### Ideas

*1* Start by listing ideas for and against your topic. Look back to *Issue 4 art 3* for ideas on how to do this.

#### The opening

*2* It is important to have a good strong opening when you write an opinion piece aimed at persuading people to change their views.

*a* You can start by presenting the opposite point of view to your own, using expressions like:

*People used to argue …*
*Some people argue …*
*According to …*

This is usually followed by linking words such as *but*, *however* or *on the other hand* which serve to introduce the other side of the argument.

---

### Glossary

**hollow:** empty, without real value

**stunted:** prevented from growing to the full (height, etc.)

**eating disorders:** illnesses which affect the diet, e.g. anorexia, an illness where a person refuses to eat properly and becomes thinner and thinner

*b* Similarly, you can start by presenting the conventional picture. You then introduce the reality using linking words like *however*. These expressions can help:

*Many people believe . . .*
*It is fashionable to think . . .*

*c* You can personalize the argument by using real examples.

*If only I'd listened . . .*
*If she had(n't) done X she would be . . .*

## Main paragraphs

3 Group what you want to say into main topic areas. Aim to devote a paragraph to each of these. Start each new paragraph with a sentence that tells the reader the main idea of the paragraph. For example:

*A related problem with sports today is the extreme competitiveness. It is not an exaggeration to say competitors may be transformed into monsters.*
*Another problem is that money has become an overriding concern . . .*

You can link additional ideas to the main topic by using expressions like *Furthermore*, *Moreover* and *In addition*.

## Closing

4 Make sure that you bring the argument to a conclusion.

*In conclusion . . .*
*To sum up . . .*

## PRACTICE

1 Use the word in brackets as part of a topic sentence for each of these paragraphs.

*a* (cheating ) Since the jobs of professionals depend on winning, they often do practically anything to win. As a result, sport becomes a vicious business. An example of this . . .

*b* (spectators) They are often obscene and violent, and fights are common at sporting events. Watching sports at home isn't problem-free either. There may be arguments . . .

*c* (injuries) Sadly most of these involve children who are introduced early in life to highly competitive sport. Medical evidence suggests . . .

2 Use the information you collected earlier to complete a paragraph introduced by the following topic sentence.

*Sport can be a very positive experience for some young people.*

### Improve your wordpower

1 Match the names of these sports to the diagrams.

volleyball   weight-lifting   fishing
table-tennis   gymnastics   archery
badminton   riding

2 Which do you think is the odd-one-out? Why?

*a* compete   train   race   play
*b* wrestling   fencing   athletics   hunting
*c* tired   depressed   stressed   injured

## WRITING

Here are some opinions on sport today.

*There's too much sport on television.*
*Sportsmen and women make too much money.*
*Winning has become too important. Look at the number of people who take drugs.*
*There's too much commercialisation in sport.*
*Events like the Olympics are too expensive.*
*It costs too much to take part and compete.*
*Sport has become something for the rich.*
*People take sport far too seriously. Just look at the behaviour of football fans.*

Use the *Improve your writing* notes to write a 140-word composition in which you discuss some of the problems of sport in modern life.

# MAKING A RADIO PROGRAMME

## WARM-UP

1  What are some of the everyday hazards for the blind and partially-sighted?
2  What sources of information are available to the blind and partially-sighted?

## TALKING POINT

You are going to produce an audio magazine programme for blind or partially-sighted teenagers. Work through these questions in a small group before you begin.

1  Decide which of these is most important in getting *you* to listen with attention and put them in order of importance.

- Interesting subjects
- Clear presentation
- Appropriate music for the introductions
- Material that is up-to-date
- Short items
- Variety of subjects
- Warm, friendly voices
- Clear introductions to each feature

  Are any of these even more important for your target group?

2  Decide on the content of your programme. Is it going to be:

- a general magazine covering a variety of topics and interests?
- a magazine dealing with a specific interest such as sport or music?

3  Take part in a meeting to plan your project. Decide on:

- the length of your programme
- the content of the programme, e.g. stories, what's on, news, interviews, etc. You may wish to look at magazines for ideas.
- who will do what to help to produce the programme
- a plan to make the programme (this should include where and when you will rehearse your presentations, record the magazine, etc.).

### Research

*Aim:*

1) to produce a radio magazine programme for blind or partially-sighted teenage learners of English.

## Hot tips!

- When the articles are ready you should meet to decide the order of presentation, how they will be introduced, etc.
- Make sure you read your presentation aloud several times before you record it, making sure that it is easy to understand and follow.
- Try to cut down on outside noise and movement when you record your tape.
- If you can get a twin-cassette machine you will find it easy to edit your tape and insert or take out sections you do not want. Many machines also have a dub facility which allows you to add background music or an extra voice.

# STREETWISE
## ISSUE 10

Gemini (22 May–21 June)

Cancer (22 June–23 July)

Taurus (21 April–21 May)

Aries (21 March–20 April)

Pisces (20 February–20 March)

## SIGNS OF THE TIMES

Libra (24 September–23 October)

Sagittarius (23 November–22 December)

(24 July–23 August)

Aquarius (21 January–19 February)

(24 August–23 September)

Scorpio (24 October–22 November)

Capricorn (23 December–20 January)

## IF MUM COULD SEE ME NOW!

## LADIES AND GENTLEMEN...

# SIGNS OF THE TIMES

## *WARM-UP*

What are the symbols on the cover of this issue? Identify your own symbol. Do you believe in horoscopes? Why/Why not?

Now repeat the names of the signs.
Make sure that you stress them correctly.

## *READING*

Read the text and answer the questions.

## HOOKED ON HOROSCOPES

Why do so many people believe in, consult, and sometimes act on the predictions of astrologers? There is no scientific evidence that it works, yet people from all backgrounds still believe in it. The question is: why?

Psychologists suggest that one answer may be the Barnum Effect. This predicts that people will accept feedback about their personality, even if it is trivial and general, when they believe it is the result of a proper procedure for assessing their personality. The suggestion is that people believe in astrology because they take the generalised descriptions, which are true of nearly everybody, to be specifically true of themselves. For example, a French astrologer sent out detailed computer horoscopes to 2,000 people. Many of the people who received them were astonished by how accurate his character analysis had been. However, he had sent exactly the same print-out to everybody. It was that of France's most famous mass-murderer!

The Barnum Effect works best in certain conditions. It is at its most powerful when people receive general feedback they believe belongs only to them. However, feedback must be favourable. This is because humans tend to be hungry for compliments, but sceptical of criticism. If the feedback is favourable with the occasional mildly negative comment (that itself may be seen as a compliment), people will believe it.

The Barnum Effect makes it easy to explain the popularity of astrology. Predictions are based on specific information such as the time and place of birth and the feedback is nearly always positive. This is especially true of the stars columns in newspapers and magazines.

This process is enhanced over time for two reasons. The first is that people selectively

*Glossary*

**trivial:**
unimportant

**Barnum Effect:**
named after
Phineas T
Barnum, a 19th-
century
American
showman and
circus owner

remember positive statements about themselves rather than negative. So people are more likely to remember feedback that coincides with their own view of themselves. Secondly, people have to pay for the services of an astrologer. If you have paid for something, you are less likely to admit you have wasted your money, and the more that one pays the better.

Astrological readings have other attractions, particularly for people who are nervous and insecure. The readings not only give useful, 'fascinating' information about oneself, but they may also predict the future so reducing anxieties and uncertainties about what will happen.

Finally, there is one other reason why people believe astrology – the self-fulfilling prophecy. The statement that 'as a Virgo, you are particularly honest', may lead to you noticing, or selectively recalling, all or any instances that confirm this behaviour (such as telling shop-keepers when they have given you too much money as change). You may then become more honest on occasions.

So beware the astrologer, and remember that we musn't believe everything that we read about ourselves, even if it is flattering. The fault of false belief is not in our stars but in ourselves.

1   Complete this summary. Use your own words where possible.

The Barnum Effect says that _____ .
The Effect works best when :

People believe statements _____ .
Feedback is _____ .

According to the Barnum Effect astrology is popular because _____ .
The other reasons astrology is popular are:

People remember _____ .
People pay astrologers and therefore _____ .
People who are uncertain want _____ .
People begin to behave _____ the horoscope predicts.

2   What do you think about the arguments you have read? Can you think of any other reasons why astrology is popular?

## *VOCABULARY*

Find words or phrases in the text which mean:

*a*   ask for advice or information
*b*   very surprised
*c*   want to have praise very much
*d*   have doubts about the truth of something
*e*   pleasing and positive
*f*   choosing carefully what they want to remember

## *must, have to, mustn't, needn't, don't have to*

Look at these examples.

Feedback *must be* favourable.
It *need not* be entirely positive.
An accurate horoscope *needs to be* drawn up.
We *mustn't* believe everything that we read.
People *have to* pay for the services of astrologers.

*a* Which sentences mean that something is necessary?
*b* Which sentence means that something is not necessary?
*c* Which sentence means that it is necessary that you do <u>not do</u> something?

## PRACTICE

1 Complete the sentences with *must*, *mustn't* and *needn't*.

*a* To complete your horoscope I ____ have your exact time of birth.

*b* You ____ read the prediction if you don't want to, but I hope you will.

*c* I want to read my stars. I ____ forget to buy a newspaper.

*d* His predictions are usually very accurate. You ____ believe him.

*e* According to my horoscope my ideal partner ____ be rich, that's not important, but he ____ be intelligent.

*f* You ____ tell me. I've already heard.

*g* Be quiet. You ____ laugh. The astrologer does not like it.

*h* I ____ try to take astrology seriously. Many of my friends believe in it.

2 Rewrite these sentences using *must*, *mustn't*, *don't have to*, and *needn't*.

Example
You are not allowed to stop here.
*You mustn't stop here.*

*a* Don't go if you don't want to.
*b* Don't smoke in class.
*c* Tidy up your room before going out.
*d* You can telephone me if you want to.
*e* Don't tell anyone anyone what the astrologer told you.
*f* It's essential that you buy her book.
*g* It isn't necessary for you to be here.

3 In every country there are actions which are thought to bring bad luck to yourself or other people. Use *must*, *mustn't* and *needn't* to write a set of social rules for a foreigner visiting your country for the first time. You should aim to answer questions like: Should I compliment a mother on a young baby? Do I need to bring an odd number of flowers?, etc.

## TALKING POINT
### Graphology

Graphology is the art of handwriting analysis. It tries to explain personality by looking at the slant and size of handwriting, how the letters are joined, dotting of *i*'s and crossing of *t*'s, etc. Although there is no scientific support for graphology, it is very popular, and more and more people use graphology to gain insights into their personality.

Work with a partner. Compare a sample of your handwriting with the examples below. Does your handwriting mirror your personality?

*Lines*
Ascending lines show optimism and descending lines show depression.
Lines close together suggest a talkative, extravagant nature. Lines very far apart indicate detachment and reserve.

*Slopes*
An extreme forward slope indicates an ambitious nature. Backward slopes indicate shyness.

forward    backward

*Loops*
Large loops below the line express an interest in material well-being (food, money, possessions, etc.).
Large loops above the line express idealism, moral values, religion, etc.

they    they

*The letter T*
Long T bars indicate leadership. Short T bars that you like to be led.

twin    twin

What are the arguments for and against using graphology and astrology? Share your opinions in a small group.

# IF MUM COULD SEE ME NOW!

## *READING* ☹

Read the text and answer the questions.

### INTO THE GAP

An increasing number of school-leavers in Britain take a gap-year between school and university. For young people this is a chance for adventure, travel and community service. It is also a chance to develop confidence, maturity and initiative. A gap-year can take many forms.

Simon Hepner went on a solo expedition across Africa and was walking along a dirt road when an elephant burst out of the bush and charged. Instinctively, the 19-year-old stood his ground. The tactic worked and the elephant halted in a cloud of dust. *Gosh, if Mum could see me now!*

Alice Elison, 18, worked in a shelter for the homeless in Washington DC, USA. One morning Alice was put in charge of making the evening meal for 1,400 people. *Oh, Mother!*

Rachel Kundra went to teach in Mexico to find that her schoolroom was nothing more than a pile of bricks. The 18-year-old Londoner promptly organized a construction programme. Hour after hour in the heat, she stood in a chain of mothers and children, passing bricks to the fathers, who built her schoolroom.

Guy Walker spent his year at London's Heathrow Airport. Terminal Two had to prepare for its busiest summer ever, and 18-year-old Guy was asked to devise and present to senior managers a detailed plan to ensure that the crowds flowed smoothly. His scheme was approved and he put it into effect. He even designed the signposting.

Gap-year adventurers arrive at college wiser and more positive. They go to university with a greater sense of purpose of what they want to achieve and they get used to being independent and living on a tight budget. In principle, universities are very much in favour of gap-years but there are two provisos. First, gap-years are not recommended for students reading maths, where continuity of study is particularly important.

Second, a gap-year must be carefully planned. It is very easy to waste the year and drift through it to delay tough decisions about the future.

Fortunately, there are numerous organizations helping school-leavers to make good use of their gap-year. They aim to fire young people with enthusiasm for careers in industry by providing challenging work experience. Guy Walker got his Heathrow job through such a scheme.

Other organizations help young people find work and adventure abroad. They offer a range of jobs from caring for blind children in Warsaw to working on Australian sheep stations. One organization runs expeditions to remote parts of the globe. Selection is tough, however, and many applicants have to raise their own funds.

There are dangers but despite tummy upsets, homesickness, loneliness and anxious moments, the gap-year is a character-shaping experience.

1. What is a gap-year?
2. How many types of gap-year are mentioned in the text?
3. Is the writer for or against gap-years? Give reasons for your answers.
4. Which one of the options mentioned appeals to you most? Why?

## *VOCABULARY*

Find words or phrases in the text which mean:

a. naturally and without thinking
b. he did not move
c. made responsible for
d. immediately and without delay
e. turn a plan into real action
f. as a general rule
g. conditions to their agreement
h. travel from place to place without a plan
i. make someone really want to do something

## *LISTENING* ☹

*Streetwise* spoke to some readers and asked them what they would do in a gap-year. Listen and complete the grid.

|  | What she/he wants to do | Why? |
|---|---|---|
| Simon Alice Alex Chris | | |

Listen again and share your answers to these questions.

Which speaker are you most sympathetic to? Why? Do you think young people should take part in community service projects abroad? Why/Why not?

### Glossary

**living on a tight budget:** living on a small amount of money

## Improve your grammar

### would rather + base form or simple past

*would rather* + base form expresses our personal preference for ourselves:

*We would rather stay in Britain*
*I would rather get on with my course.*

Or someone else's personal preference for themselves:

*He would rather eat chicken than beef.*

*would rather* can also be used to express what we want someone else to do. In this case *would rather* is followed by a simple past verb (but with a present or future meaning).

*I would rather you stayed here.*
*My parents would rather I went somewhere in Europe . . .*

### It's time + simple past

When we want to say that 'it's time' for ourselves or somebody else to do something, we often use the structure *It's time* + subject + past-tense verb (with a present or future meaning).

*It's time we did something for the poorer countries . . .*

*It's time* can also be followed by a base form with *to*.

*It's time to go.*

This has a similar present/future meaning to *It's time we left.*

## PRACTICE 1

1  Complete these sentences with an appropriate verb.

a  My parents would rather I _____ at home.
b  We would rather _____ to the United States.
c  He has just joined the army. His parents would rather he _____ a job in a bank.
d  He would rather _____ tea than coffee.

2  Write a sentence with *I'd/We'd rather . . .* or *It's time . . .* for each situation.

a  Your teacher suggests that you spend a year learning German. You would like to go to China.
b  You want to spend a year on an expedition to the Amazon. Your parents suggest that you work in your father's law firm.

c  A friend has a place in two universities. One is to study engineering. The other is to study medicine. Term starts next week.
d  You are offered a part-time job in a library or a record shop. What is your choice?
e  You are offered a place on a year-long expedition to the South Pole or the Sahara Desert. What would your parents say?
f  You are a brilliant maths student. You want to spend a gap-year working in a hospital. What would your teacher say?

## GETTING STREETWISE!  😀

### Advice

Listen to this conversation.

1  What does the first speaker want to know?
2  What expressions does she use to give advice?
3  How does her friend respond?
4  Listen and repeat with the same intonation.

## Use and usage

### had better

We use *had better* (or *'d better*) to say what is the best thing to do in a situation.
*He's doing badly. He'd better work harder.*
*Had better* is stronger than *should/ought to.*

## PRACTICE 2

1  Complete the sentences.

a  Sam's late again. Has he thought of _____ ?
b  You're leaving next week. You had better _____ preparing for your trip!
c  'I can't sleep.' 'Have you tried _____ ?'
d  The train is coming. You'd better _____ .
e  You seem to be having a problem with maths. Have you thought of _____ ?

2  Imagine that you are the people in the cartoon. Develop a conversation in which you reject your friend's advice. Use as many expressions for giving and responding to advice as you can.

Have you ever thought of getting a job in the city?

# LADIES AND GENTLEMEN...

## WARM-UP

Complete this questionnaire individually.

You have to speak in English to a group of strangers. Would you ...

| | Yes | No |
|---|---|---|
| be frightened? | | |
| become self-conscious? | | |
| forget what you wanted to say? | | |
| be afraid of making mistakes? | | |
| lack self-confidence? | | |

Share your answers in a small group. Talk about why you would feel that way and describe any experiences you have had with public speaking.

Rank these criteria for a good talk from the most important to the least important.

- audible
- clear and easy to follow
- short
- interesting
- amusing
- the speaker was interested in the topic

Share your conclusions and agree on the three most important criteria for a good talk.

## LISTENING

Fear of public speaking is perfectly normal and affects most people. *Streetwise* decided to look at some ways to overcome this fear. Listen and note the four main points.

## PRONUNCIATION
### Stress

In a speech it is important to stress the important words.

1 Practise reading these lines trying to make the ideas clear and convincing.

> If you think you are beaten, you are.
> If you think you dare not, you don't.
> If you'd like to win, but think you can't,
> It's almost certain you won't.
> Life's battles don't always go
> To the stronger or faster person.
> Sooner or later the person who wins
> Is the one who thinks she can.

2 Listen to a reading on the tape and mark the main stress. How was it the same or different from your own reading?

## *Improve your writing*

### Writing a talk

Although few of us become public speakers most of us will have to address a group of people at some time.

*a* Start by noting down everything you have to say. Think about who you are talking to and how much they know about the subject and divide your points into those you have to say and those you can miss out without ruining the talk. This will help you to avoid trying to say too much.

*b* Think of a good start. Many people start with a formula like:

*Good afternoon, Ladies and gentlemen. My name is ... The topic of my talk today is ...*

or you may prefer to use a quotation, or tell an anecdote. However, you should always preview what you are going to say:

*I would like to talk about ...*
*I am going to talk about ...*

*c* Make sure you have a structure for what you want to say. If you are talking about personal experience, such as a hobby, you may wish to follow this structure:

*The past*: when, why, and how you started.

*The present*: what you do, when, and where.

*The future*: possible developments, your hopes and ambitions.

*d*  In the body of the talk you should separate your main points. You can use links such as:

*First of all ..., Next ..., Finally ...*
*First, second, third*
*My main point is ...*

*e*  Make sure that your talk has an ending. You may wish to give a quick summary of what you have said.

*In conclusion, let me remind you ...*
*I'm sure you agree that ...*

## PRACTICE

**1**  Put these extracts from a welcome talk into the best order.

After that, we'll look round the school together.
Ladies and gentlemen, it gives me great pleasure to welcome you to our school.
Let me remind you that in the first part of our programme our head teacher will give you a short talk on the history of the school.
My name is Jose Manuel and I will be your guide this afternoon.
I hope you enjoy your visit and if you follow me I'll show you to your talk.

**2**  Fill in each of the blanks with one of the following expressions:

*My reason for talking to you*
*Ladies and gentlemen*
*In addition to that*
*I would like to begin*
*Finally*
*However*
*Before I end*
*I am sure you will agree that*
*The main reason*

Good morning ____ (*a*). My name is Daniel Boon and I am President of an unusual club. ____ (*b*) by telling you a little bit about our club.

In 1982 the founder of our club threw himself from a bridge which was 320m above the Arkansas river. It's alright, he was attached to the bridge by 260 m of elastic rope and he was fine when they rescued him two hours later!! The name of our club is the Dangerous Sports Club and the aim of our club is to 'act boldly in an overprotected world.' ____ (*c*) today is to ask you for your support and help. But why help us?

____ (*d*) is that some of our activities are really very serious. For example, at present two of our members are travelling up the Amazon with medical supplies.

____ (*e*) our activities provide our sponsors with a lot of publicity. There are only thirty of us but we have been in the newspapers, magazines and television fifty times in the last year. You are welcome to look at the material in the exhibition.

____ (*f*), we need your help in our mission to make the world a less boring place.

____ (*g*) I would like to tell you something about our plans for next year. One group hopes to walk to the South Pole, another will climb Everest without oxygen, another will try to climb the Eiffel Tower.

____ (*h*) all this depends on you because we need your money. ____ (*i*) we are a deserving if unusual cause. So please give generously.

## WRITING

The aim is to prepare a short talk about something that you are interested in talking about. Choose A or B:

A  Give a talk on something you are interested in, such as a hobby, e.g. karate, model-making, etc.

B  Give a talk about something that you feel strongly about, e.g. smoking, traffic problems, pollution, etc.

In either case you need to:

*a*  have clear aims and objectives, e.g. to tell people about your hobby so that they can take it up or to convert people to your point of view.

*b*  follow the guide-lines in the *Improve your writing* section.

*c*  bear in mind the criteria for a good talk that you looked at in the *Warm-up*.

# POP

## *READING*

Read the text and answer the questions.

### CHARACTERISTICS OF POP SONG LYRICS

I love you,
Do you love
me, baby?

Do these lyrics seem familiar? A recent analysis of 50 pop songs in English revealed the following:

- Pop songs are very personal. Almost all pop songs use *I*.
- 88% use *you*, but the referent is rarely mentioned by name.
- The major theme is *love* and the stereotypical message of most songs is *I love you*, but we are never told who *I* and *you* are.
- Only 6 out of 50 song lyrics mention the sex of the singer and only 17 mention the sex of *you*.
- 94% of the songs mention no time reference and 80% have no place reference in order to make their appeal universal.
- Furthermore, the universal appeal is heightened by the fact that many pop singer's voices are neither distinctively male nor female.

1    Do you agree with the above analysis of pop songs? Do your favourite songs fit the description?
2    List the characteristics of pop songs in your language.

## *LISTENING*  😐

### The language of pop

Pop songs are frequently criticized for their use of slang and non-standard expressions. It is true that words like *gimme*, *ain't*, *gonna*, *wanna*, are very common in pop song lyrics. But pop lyrics can also make a lasting contribution to our language. Consider the following:

All you need is love
　　　　　Give peace a chance
Blowing in the wind
　　　　　Don't think twice, it's all right

Listen to Stephen Frazer's report before answering the questions.

1    Who do the lyrics belong to?
2    What book have they recently appeared in?
3    Why were these lyrics chosen?
4    Rewrite the following pop lyrics in standard English.

*a*    You ain't nothin' but a hound-dog
*b*    Never gonna give you up, never gonna let you down
*c*    I wanna dance with somebody
*d*    We gotta get out while we're young, 'Cause tramps like us, Baby, we were born to run
*e*    I ain't gonna work on Maggie's Farm no more.

## *TALKING POINT*

Read this extract from one of Bob Dylan's songs entitled *The Times They are A-Changing*.

Come mothers and fathers
Throughout the land
And don't criticize
What you can't understand
Your sons and your daughters
Are beyond your command
Your old road is
Rapidly agin'
Please get out of the new one
If you can't lend a hand
For the times they are a-changin'!

1    What is the sentiment behind the song? Do you agree with it? Why/Why not?
2    Do you feel that the lyrics of pop songs can set a bad example to young people?

### Research

*Aim:*

1)    to select memorable lines from well-known songs and use them in a quiz where the other students have to identify the original song and/or the pop group or singer. These can be translations of songs in your own language.

# GRAMMAR REVIEW ISSUES 9 AND 10

## THIRD CONDITIONAL
### Form

*If* + past perfect + *would have* + past participle
short form: *'d* (= *had/would*)

| Uses | Examples |
|---|---|
| 1  To talk about an event that did not happen because of the condition in the *if* clause. The third conditional is often used for excuses. | *If I had gone, the other bloke would have taken the picture.* (I didn't go, so I took the picture and the other man didn't.) *If I'd had the money, I would have given them some.* (I didn't, so I didn't give them any.) |
| 2  To talk about a condition that is unreal because it did not and could not happen. | *If I had been born a hundred years ago, I would have had a different life.* |

### Note

The *if* clause can appear in the second part of the sentence. No comma is used.
*I wouldn't have come if I'd known you were busy.*

## THIRD CONDITIONAL WITH PRESENT OUTCOME
### Form

| *If* clause | main clause |
|---|---|
| Imagined condition past perfect | Present outcome *would* + base form |

### Example

*If Shirley had worn a helmet, she wouldn't have problems with her sight now.* (But she didn't, so she has.)

| Use | Example |
|---|---|
| To talk about the present result of an imagined past action. | *If I had worked hard in school, I wouldn't be unemployed.* (But I didn't, so I am.) |

## WISH/IF ONLY + PAST PERFECT

*Wish* or *If only* + past perfect express regret for something that did or didn't happen in the past.
*I wish I had learned to play the guitar.* (. . . but I didn't learn to play it.)
*If only I hadn't failed my exam.* (. . . but I failed it.)

### Note

We can't use *would have* for past regrets.
*I wish you had told me.* (NOT I wish you would have told me.)

## MUST, NEED, HAVE TO

| Uses | Examples |
|---|---|
| 1  Use both *must* and *have to* to express obligation or necessity. | *I must go, my father is waiting.* *I have to be home by ten.* |
| 2  Use *needn't, don't need to, haven't got to* or *don't have to* + base form to say that it is not necessary to do something. | *I don't need to go to school tomorrow, it's Sunday.* *I haven't got to go to school tomorrow, . . .* *I needn't go . . .* *I don't have to go . . .* |
| 3  Use *mustn't* when there is an obligation not to do something. | *You mustn't sit here.* (= Do not sit here.) |

## WOULD RATHER

1 *Would rather* + base form expresses our personal preference for ourselves.
   *I would rather get on with my course.*
   *We would rather stay in Britain.*
   *He would rather have chicken.*

2 *Would rather* can also express what we want someone else to do. In this case it is followed by a verb in the simple past (with a present or future meaning).
   *My parents would rather I went to India.*
   *I would rather you stayed here.*

## IT'S TIME + SIMPLE PAST

When we want to say that it's time for ourselves or somebody else to do something, we often use the structure *It's time* + subject + simple past (with a present or future meaning).
*It's time we did something for poorer countries.*
*It's time you started revising for the exam.*

### Note

*It's time* can also be followed by the base form with *to*.
*It's time to go* is similar to *It's time we left.*

## HAD BETTER

We use *had better* to say what is the best thing to do in a situation, or to give advice. It is followed by the base form. Although we use *had* in this structure, the meaning is present or future, not past.

*We're making too much noise! We had better turn the music down.*
*You'd better wear your seat belt.*

---

# GRAMMAR PRACTICE

## A

1 Put the verb in brackets in an appropriate form.
Example
I *wouldn't have done* (do) it if I had known.

a She wouldn't have known if you _____ (not tell) her.

b We _____ (win) the match if you had played better.

c Would you have helped if you _____ (be) him?

d I enjoyed the party but I _____ (not go) if you hadn't asked me.

e They _____ (arrive) earlier if they hadn't missed the bus.

f I would have come to see you if I _____ (not leave) your address at home.

g My mother _____ (not buy) me the shoes even if she had had the money. She really didn't like them.

2 Put in *must*, *mustn't*, or *needn't*.

a I'm sorry I can't speak to you now. I _____ finish my homework.

b The president has given everyone a special holiday, so we _____ go to work tomorrow.

c I was late for school yesterday. I _____ be late again today.

d The library has asked me for the books I borrowed. I _____ return them.

e You _____ buy her a gift for her birthday. She isn't expecting one from you.

f When I was young I was told that I _____ play with matches.

g The film was great! You _____ go and see it.

3 Complete the sentences using *had better* and one of the verbs from the list.

repair   wear   go   apologise   buy

a My tyre is flat. I _____ it.

b The police are checking motorcyclists. You _____ your helmet.

c It's your exam tomorrow. You _____ to bed early.

d The tape-recorder needs new batteries. You _____ some.

e She's very angry with them. They _____ to her.

## B

1 Read each situation and write a sentence with *if*.
Example
She didn't go because she was ill.
*If she hadn't been ill, she would have gone.*

a I didn't speak to her because I didn't see her.

b He didn't buy the book because it was very expensive.

c She wasn't injured because she wore a helmet.

d The plants died because he didn't water them.

e I didn't watch the programme because I didn't know it was on.

f They got lost because the weather was bad.

**2** Read each situation and write a sentence with *if*, using the third conditional with a present result.

Example
She is ill because she ate too much.
*If she hadn't eaten too much she wouldn't be ill.*

*a* She is in hospital because she fell off a horse.
*b* He is at medical school because he passed all his exams.
*c* My uncle speaks fluent French because he learnt it as a child.
*d* She is alive because the doctors were able to help her.
*e* He lives in Australia because his parents moved there when he was a young boy.
*f* He is a lot thinner because he has been on diet.

**3** Finish the sentences so that they mean the same as the sentence before. Use *must*, *mustn't* and *needn't*.

*a* It is not necessary for me to go to school tomorrow because it is a holiday.
I _____ .
*b* It is essential to stop when you see this sign.
You _____ .
*c* Smoking is forbidden here.
You _____ .
*d* It is very important to study before important exams.
You _____ .
*e* I don't have to change buses to get to his house.
I _____ .
*f* Playing loud music in public is against the law in the UK.
In the UK, you _____ .

**4** Put the verbs in an appropriate form.

Example
I would rather you *went* (go) instead of me.

*a* I'd rather you _____ (stay) here.
*b* We needn't _____ (hurry). The bus doesn't leave yet.
*c* I would rather they _____ (tell) me about it.
*d* I wish you _____ (stop) chewing your nails.
*e* We'd better _____ (discuss) this another time.
*f* It's time we _____ (finish) this exercise.

**5** Complete the sentences using an appropriate verb in the past perfect.

remember   buy   eat   wear   study

*a* I feel ill. If only _____ .
*b* My girlfriend is furious with me because I forgot her birthday. I wish _____ .
*c* She got badly sunburnt at the beach. She wishes _____ .
*d* He failed his exams, so now he wishes _____ .
*e* Those computers were very cheap and now they're expensive. I wish _____ .

**6** Use the pictures to help you to complete the sentences.

Example
*a* I would rather *wear red than black*.
*b* I would rather _____ .
*c* My parents would rather I _____ .
*d* I'd rather _____ .
*e* The sports teacher would rather you _____ .
*f* I would rather _____ .

# C

**1** Complete these sentences to show how life would have been different if you had been born as a member of the opposite sex.

*If I had been born a ...      I wouldn't be ...*
*My parents would have ...    I would have ...*
*My name ...                  I wouldn't have ...*

**2** Use *I wish* or *If only* + past perfect to list six things that you regret about your life to date.

**3** Imagine that some friends are coming to visit you this winter. This is part of their letter.
'What clothes should we bring? Do we need an overcoat? What about an umbrella? Is there anything else you would like us to bring?'
Use *must*, *mustn't* and *needn't* to write a paragraph replying to their question.

# *Wise up!*

# SPEAKING

## HOW TO KEEP GOING

There may be times when you become uncertain while you are speaking English. You can help yourself by:

- asking for help if you haven't understood.
  Use questions like *Do you want me to...?* or *Did you say...?*, and checking with rising intonation such as *Cars?* These create a much better impression than silence, or noises like *Uh?*
- giving yourself time to think.
  Use expressions like *I'm not sure but...* or *I think that...* as well as *Well/I mean/Erm.*
- using alternatives for words you do not know.
  Use expressions like

  *It's a kind of...*
  *It's a sort of...*
  *It's a thing for...*

- using other strategies, like gestures.

1  Work in pairs or groups and list some of the strategies you use in your own language? Are you conscious of them? Do you use them in English? Are there any that you use too often?

## CREATE A GOOD IMPRESSION

When you are speaking English you can create a good impression if you SOFTEN.

| | |
|---|---|
| S | = Smile |
| O | = be Open (show that you want to talk) |
| F | = lean Forward |
| T | = Try your best |
| E | = make Eye contact with the people you are speaking to |
| N | = Nod to show you are listening and following |

1  How important are each of these areas in your own culture? For example, is eye contact important? Do you have alternatives to nodding?
2  Work with a partner. Try what it feels like if you SOFTEN. Now try the opposite. Who would you prefer to talk to? Why?

## WHAT THE EXAMINER WANTS

A speaking exam is designed to get a sample of your spoken language. To do this examiners may:

- ask you specific questions.
- get you to describe a picture.
- ask you to respond to a situation, e.g. 'You are in a restaurant and want to order a meal. What do you say?'
- ask you to solve a problem.
- get you to talk about a project or set book.

As you talk they will give you marks in areas such as:

- fluency or the ability to keep a conversation going.
- grammatical accuracy or correctness.
- pronunciation, including sounds, stress, and intonation.
- vocabulary – using a range of words and finding your way round problems.
- You may also be assessed on your ability to complete a task.

1  Find out about the requirements of any oral exam you may take. How many parts does it have? What tasks does it use to get you talking? How long does it usually take? Which aspects of the exam do you need further practice in?

2  Look at these statements. Are there any which apply especially to you? Discuss your conclusions in a small group.

a  I often have to repeat what I have just said because people don't understand me.
b  I find it very difficult to say what I want to say.
c  I don't mind making mistakes when I speak.
d  I think my accent in English is terrible.
e  I am never lost for words. I always find some way to say what I want.
f  I find it easy to talk to other people.

3  Work with a partner.

   **Student A** – Take the role of an examiner. Ask your partner to talk about one of the cover pictures in *Streetwise*. Use expressions like *Tell me about...*, *What do you think of...?*, *Do you like/dislike...?*, *Do you agree/disagree?*, etc. to get your partner to talk. See if your partner uses the strategies you have been reading about.

   **Student B** – Imagine you are a candidate. You must respond appropriately to your partner, but use the strategies you have been reading about to say as much as possible.

   When both of you have finished, discuss how you can improve.

# STREETWISE

## ISSUE 11

**SO MUCH FOR ROMANCE**

Her story

His story

**THE RIGHT TO FIGHT**

**TRUE STORIES**

# SO MUCH FOR ROMANCE

## WARM-UP

Share your answers to these questions.
Where would you go if you went out on a first date with someone of the opposite sex? Who would pay for what? Why?

## READING 😦

Read this story about a blind date. As you read the text, decide what went wrong at each stage.

### BLIND DATE

### The phone call

*Her story*

Sam got my name from a friend. He telephoned me and invited me to see a film. I accepted, but although I explained that it was time for my piano practice, he started talking about himself, and there was no stopping him. I couldn't have got in a word edgewise even if I had wanted to!

*His story*

Susan is a friend of George. He told me that she was really pretty and had a lovely personality, so I rang her and asked her for a date. I was delighted when she agreed but it was really difficult talking to her. She wouldn't say a word. I had to carry on the whole conversation myself.

### The arrival

*Her story*

When he came to pick me up, I was getting ready. When I came to the door and saw the ridiculous outfit he was wearing, I almost died of embarrassment. Then he suggested that we took a bus. I didn't know where to look.

*His story*

I got there on time. Her Mum answered the door and asked me what I wanted. I explained that I was Susan's date. I think she was impressed by my suit, and you should have seen Susan's face when she first came to the door! As we walked to the bus stop she grumbled that Damian always took her out by car. I told her she looked lovely!

*Glossary*

**blind date:** a date is an appointment to go out with a member of the opposite sex. You go on a blind date if you have never met your partner before.

### The movie

*Her story*

He laughed so loudly that everybody turned round to look at us. I whispered 'be quiet' several times but it had no effect. He also made a loud noise eating his popcorn. I wanted to crawl into a hole.

*His story*

She was a real bore. The film was very funny, but she kept muttering throughout. She refused everything that I offered her.

### The meal

*Her story*

He took me to a hamburger restaurant, and insisted on ordering a whole meal for me. It was awful. I wasn't even hungry.

*His story*

She let me order the most expensive dish on the menu and she didn't even touch a bite. She explained that she was still full from lunch, but I think she wanted to go somewhere more expensive. She's a real snob.

### The future

*Her story*

Would I go out with him again? You must be joking. I never want to see him again. He was so insensitive.

*His story*

I would never call her again. She behaved terribly, and never apologized. One date with her was more than enough.

Answer the questions.

1 Sam and Susan do not want to see each other again. Why? Use your own words to describe the reasons from Sam's and Susan's own points of view.

2 Do you think the date could have gone better? How? What could each of them have done?

## VOCABULARY

Look back at the introduction and text.

1 Find expressions that mean:
a find it difficult to say anything
b I was really embarrassed (There are 3.)

2 What is the meaning of the expressions in **bold**?

a saw the **ridiculous** outfit he was wearing
 i strange
 ii deserving to be laughed at

*b* she **was impressed** by my suit
  *i* she was shocked by the suit
  *ii* she admired the suit

*c* she **grumbled** that Damian always took her out by car
  *i* complained in a bad-tempered way
  *ii* spoke softly

*d* I **whispered** be quiet
  *i* said something very quietly using only breath
  *ii* made a loud sound by forcing breath through your lips

*e* She kept **muttering**
  *i* smiling and being cheerful
  *ii* complaining quietly

*f* a real **snob**
  *i* a person who thinks they have superior tastes, knowledge, etc.
  *ii* a person who dislikes people who are different from them

*g* He's so **insensitive**
  *i* lacking in reason and good sense
  *ii* unaware of other people's feelings

## Grammar quiz

### Reported speech

1 *She explained that she was still full from lunch.*

   What were the original words?
   What happens to tenses in reported speech?

2 *Would you like to go to a film?*
   *What time shall we meet?*

   Decide how you would report these questions if you wanted to report the original words.

3 Sometimes a writer uses a verb to give us an idea of what was said, but does not report the exact words. For example, in the first part of Susan's story we have *He telephoned and invited me to see a film, I accepted* and *He started talking about himself.* How many other examples can you find?

## PRACTICE

1 Rewrite these sentences so that you keep the same meaning. Start with the words given.

*a* 'Why do we have to go by bus?'
   She complained about _____ .
*b* 'Would you like to go to a film?'
   He invited _____ .
*c* 'Waiter! Two coffees, please.'
   He ordered _____ .
*d* 'I don't want one.'
   I _____ .
*e* 'I'm not hungry.'
   I _____ .

2 Use these verbs to give your reader a sense of what was said in the following conversations.

   offer   insist   apologize   explained
   complain   accept   agree   suggest

Leslie: Would you like to have a coffee?
Sarah:  Yes, please.
Leslie: Here you are!
Sarah:  It's cold and horrible!
Leslie: I'm terribly sorry. I'll make some more.

Andy: How about going to the cinema?
Pete:  I'm sorry I can't. I've got a lot of homework.
Andy: Oh come on! Of course you can.
Pete:  All right, I'll come with you.

## PRONUNCIATION
### Tone of voice

When we are writing we often use verbs like whisper, moan, mumble, etc. to give an idea of how something was said. Work in pairs and decide how you would read these sentences.

*a* 'Be quiet!' she whispered.
*b* 'No!' he bellowed.
*c* 'Ssh,' she said softly.
*d* 'I don't like it here,' he moaned.
*e* 'Don't be silly!' she laughed.

Now listen to the tape and repeat the sentences in the same way.

## WRITING

Write the story of a real or imaginary first date. You should include information about:

- who the person was, and where you met
- where you went
- how the date went (What did you talk about? Did you get on? Why/ Why not?)
- the future (Do you think you will see the person again? Why/Why not?)

# THE RIGHT TO FIGHT

## WARM-UP

Why do people box?
Would you let your child be a boxer?

## LISTENING

David 'Awesome' Lawrence is a New York businessman. He is a millionaire with a PhD in English Literature. He also boxes for fun, and he has recently turned professional.

*Streetwise* decided to find out why he boxes. Try and predict his answer before listening to the interview.

Choose the best answer to each question.

1 David boxes because
  a he is a powerful businessman.
  b he has nothing left to achieve.
  c it teaches him about himself.
  d it teaches him about people.

2 David started boxing
  a for charity.
  b to make money.
  c to become fit.
  d to learn about himself.

3 David thinks the main reason poor kids box is
  a for money.
  b to change their situation.
  c to overcome prejudice.
  d they like fighting.

4 David's son
  a approves of boxing.
  b goes to his father's fights.
  c broke his nose in training.
  d disapproves of boxing.

5 David's son made a pile of the boxing clothes because
  a David had decided to quit.
  b David was finished.
  c he wanted David to stop.
  d he was feeling miserable.

6 David thinks boxing
  a helps him relax.
  b is not dangerous.
  c can't cause brain damage.
  d hasn't changed his life.

## VOCABULARY

Match the words to the definitions.

| cowardice | struggle | ghetto | quit |
| thrill | solemnly | prejudice | |

a sudden feeling of great excitement
b very seriously
c opinion that is not founded on experience or reason
d area of town or city where many poor people or people of a particular race, nationality or religion live in isolation from the majority
e stop doing something; give up
f behaviour of a person who lacks courage or runs away from dangerous things
g effort which is very difficult and where you have to try hard

## Improve your grammar

### Gerund and infinitive

*He **refuses** to come to any of my fights.*
*Lawrence **enjoys** fighting...*

If we want to follow *refuse* with a verb, the second verb must be an infinitive (base form with *to*).
If we want to follow *enjoy* with a verb, the second verb must be a gerund (*-ing* form).

Some verbs can take either an *-ing* form or infinitive with *to* with no difference in meaning: *start, begin, continue, intend. People started to leave* (Or *started leaving*) *before the disco was over.*

However, we do not usually have two *-ing* forms together.
*It was starting to rain.* (NOT It was starting raining.)

A few verbs take *-ing* or an infinitive with *to* with a change of meaning, e.g. *stop, remember, try, go on.*

What is the difference in meaning between these examples?
a Although his family didn't like it, he went on fighting.
b He began by boxing for fun but then he went on to become a professional.

## PRACTICE 1

**1** Complete the sentences putting the verb in brackets into either the gerund or the infinitive with *to*.

*a* David refuses ____ (give up) boxing.

*b* Do you enjoy ____ (fight)?

*c* David hopes ____ (continue) as a boxer.

*d* I finished ____ (train) last week.

*e* He gave up ____ (box) years ago.

*f* fo you ever feel like ____ (go) to fights?

*g* I offered ____ (help) him.

*h* I forgot ____ (visit) him before I went home.

*i* After he had left school he went on ____ (train) as a teacher.

**2** Write each pair of sentences as one. Use the -*ing* form or a *to-* infinitive.

Example
It was time to have coffee. So the workers stopped.
*The workers stopped to have coffee.*

*a* He had been training for hours. But he went on.
He _____ .

*b* He didn't want to go to the gym any more. So he stopped.
He _____ .

*c* He wanted to post a letter. He stopped on the way home.
He _____ .

*d* Alice didn't bring her text book. She forgot.
Alice _____ .

*e* He wanted to try and get fit. He went to the gym.
He tried _____ .

*f* I visited Disneyland when I was twelve. I'll never forget it,
I'll never_____ .

## GETTING STREETWISE! 😦

### Predictions

We asked the *Streetwise* panel if they thought boxing would ever disappear.

**1** Listen and match the names of the panel to the expressions used to introduce their main predictions.

| Names | Expressions |
|---|---|
| Mike | I think its bound to be … |
| Sandra | I think it's unlikely … |
| Alex | I'm sure it would … |
| Alan | I wouldn't be surprised if … |

**2** Listen to the tape again. This time, summarise the views of each panel member.

| | Predicts | Reason |
|---|---|---|
| **Mike** | | |
| **Alex** | | |
| **Sandra** | | |
| **Alan** | | |

**3** Which panel member do you agree with most? Why?

## PRACTICE 2

**1** Look at these expressions. They are all ways of making predictions and they all answer the question: *Do you think he'll hurt himself if he starts boxing?*

*He's unlikely to hurt himself much.*
*I bet you (that) he'll hurt himself.*
*He's bound to hurt himself.*
*I doubt if he'll do himself much harm.*
*I suppose he might injure himself.*
*There's not much chance of him suffering serious injury.*
*I wouldn't be surprised if he hurt himself.*

Find the expressions which suggest that the speaker thinks the prediction is very likely. Now, order the predictions from the likely to the unlikely.

**2** Use the expressions to write your predictions on the future of these sports in your country in the next twenty years.

boxing   golf   tennis   basketball
cricket   American football

Example
*I bet you that American football will become more popular.*

# TRUE STORIES

## READING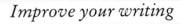
Read the text and answer the questions.

### EXPLOSION IN THE PARLOUR

The host poured tea into the cup and placed it on the small table in front of his guests, who were a father and daughter, and put the lid on the cup with a clink. Apparently thinking of something, he hurried into the inner room, leaving the thermos on the table. His guests heard a chest of drawers opening.

They remained in the parlour, the ten-year-old daughter looking at the flowers outside the window, the father just about to take his cup, when the crash came, right there in the parlour. Something was hopelessly broken.

It was the thermos, which had fallen to the floor. The girl looked over her shoulder abruptly, startled, staring. It was mysterious. Neither of them had touched it, not even a little bit. True, it hadn't stood steadily when their host placed it on the table, but it hadn't fallen then.

The crash of the thermos caused the host, with a box of sugar cubes in his hand, to rush back from the inner room. He stared at the steaming floor and blurted out, 'It doesn't matter! It doesn't matter!'

The father started to say something. Then he muttered, 'Sorry, I touched it and it fell.'

'It doesn't matter,' the host said.

Later, when they left the house, the daughter said, 'Daddy, *did* you touch it?'

'No. But it stood so close to me.'

'But you *didn't* touch it. I saw your reflection in the window-pane. You were sitting perfectly still.'

The father laughed. 'What then would you give as the cause of its fall?'

'The thermos fell by itself. The floor is uneven. It wasn't steady when Mr Li put it there. Daddy, *why* did you say that you ...'

'That won't do, girl. It sounds more acceptable when I say I knocked it down. There are things which people accept less the more you defend them. The truer the story you tell, the less true it sounds.'

The daughter was lost in silence for a while. Then she said, 'Can you explain it only this way?'

'Only this way,' her father said.

1 Do we know how and why the thermos fell to the ground?

2 Do you think the father did the right thing? What would you have done and said?

3 Do you agree with the statement 'the truer the story you tell, the less true it sounds'? Can you give any examples of true stories which were not believed, or times when it has been easier *not* to tell the truth?

### Glossary

**thermos:** container used to keep hot drinks hot and cold drinks cold

**parlour:** sitting room (old fashioned)

## *Improve your writing*

### Direct and indirect speech in narrative

Lively narrative often contains a mixture of direct and indirect speech.

1 If you are using direct speech remember the punctuation rules.

a Each piece of speech is enclosed by inverted commas.

b Every new piece of speech must begin with a capital letter.

c Each piece of speech must end with a full stop or an exclamation mark or a question mark *before* the concluding inverted commas ...

d ... unless the sentence is going to continue, when it ends with a comma. This also comes *before* the concluding inverted commas.

e When a piece of speech comes in the middle of a sentence it must have a comma (or sometimes a colon) just before the opening inverted commas.

f Start a new line for each speaker.

Look back at the text and find examples of each of these rules.

2 When we use indirect speech in normal communication we often summarize the main points of a conversation. In writing a story we can do the same.

*She suggested that we went out together.*

## PRACTICE

Rewrite these passages so that you use a mix of narrative and direct speech. Remember to use the correct punctuation and layout.

*a* When I was twelve I was not a great lover of school. One morning, I decided that I would rather take the day off school, so when I got downstairs I told my Mum that I had a stomach-ache. However, my Mum didn't believe me, and told me if I really had stomach-ache then I'd have to go to the doctor's, hoping this would scare me into going to school. It didn't! I went to the doctor's and the doctor did believe me. He believed me so much he sent me to hospital!

*b* Alan came into the room. His face was white. I asked him what had happened. He just pointed at the ruined building. Later when he calmed down he told me that he had been there alone and the lift had suddenly begun to go up. There hadn't been any sound – and it was very strange. I told him he was being silly and laughed at him. I felt strange when Alan quietly said that there was no way the lift could have been moved mechanically. There was no power and electricity and the brake was on.

## Use and usage

### Adverbs

Some adverbs can be used in an initial position to modify a whole sentence. These include adverbs of manner such as *quietly, gently, slowly, happily*, etc. We use them for dramatic effect, or to create suspense. They are followed by a comma.

*Alan stood still and held his breath. Slowly, he went towards the lift.*

Perform the action in the second sentence in the manner of an adverb of your choice. See if the other students can guess what the adverb is.

*a* She took the baby in her arms. _____ , she combed its hair.

*b* Sheila got the best marks in the class. _____ , she went home to tell her mother.

*c* I showed her the letter from her father. _____ , she read it.

## WRITING 1

Imagine you were the girl in the story. You decide to write a contribution to a magazine, telling the story of your father and thermos.

- Start by describing the incident and where it happened.
- Talk about the initial reaction of the people there.
- Highlight your confusion, your father's explanation, and what it has meant for you since then.

Use a mixture of direct and indirect speech. Begin '*When I was ten I remember...*'

## LISTENING

BBC Radio 1, which is one of the most popular national pop music stations, has a series of true-life revelations on its breakfast show. These take the form of listeners' confessions to Simon Mayo who is a popular DJ. Listen to these confessions and decide:

*a* whether the writer should be forgiven.

*b* which story is more believable.

Be ready to give your reasons.

## WRITING 2

Work in pairs and think of as many explanations for this incident as possible.

*A young person offers to walk his mother's favourite dog. He sets off with the dog and his sister. The dog disappears mysteriously during the walk. He and his sister are left with it's lead.*

*Either*

Imagine you were involved and write a 'true' confession about the incident:

- Start by introducing the subject of your confession.
- Tell the story. Use a new paragraph for each of the main events. If there is any speech, use a mixture of direct and indirect speech.
- End by saying who you want forgiveness from, and why.

*Or*

Build the incident into a 'strange but true' story along the lines of 'Explosion in the parlour'. Refer back to *Issue 3 part 3* for guidelines on 'viewpoint'.

# POETRY POSTERS

## *READING*

### HAIKU

Haiku is a form of poetry that originated in Japan. Haiku poems follow set rules:

- A haiku has three lines and seventeen syllables.
- There are normally five syllables in the first line, seven in the second and five in the third.
- It contains some reference to nature.
- It refers to a specific event that is happening now, not in the past.

1   Read these examples of haiku and decide if they follow the rules.

Gold, brown, and red leaves
All twirling and scattering
As the children play.

Sunset: carrying
a red balloon, he looks back...
a child leaves the zoo.

Snow melts,
and the village is overflowing -
with children.

2   Which of these haiku do you like best? Why?

## DEFINITION POEMS

Read the last verse of a poem by Adrian Henri entitled *Love is...*

Love is you and love is me
Love is a prison and love is free
Love's what's there when you're away from me
Love is...

1   Answer the questions.
a   How does every line start?
b   What do the last words in each complete line have in common?
c   What is the poet trying to do in this poem?

2   Work in groups. Each member of the group should provide their own definition of one of these topics:

Friendship... Freedom... Hate... School... Life...

Continue until you run out of ideas. Refine the ideas, and see if you can produce your own definition poem.

### Research

*Aim:*

1)   to produce a poetry poster to illustrate and display a poem you have written.

### *Hot tips!*

- Spend a few minutes writing down all the images and ideas you have before you begin.
- Try to 'find' poems in other forms of writing such as travel brochures, descriptive articles, newspaper items, etc. Choose a text that is relevant to your theme and highlight and list interesting words and expressions. Select material and ideas to build into a poem.
- Look for a picture to write about and make that into a poster. For example, you could write a haiku based on a picture of nature.
- Alternatively draw, or choose from magazines, pictures to illustrate a poem you have already written.

# STREETWISE

## ISSUE 12

## EUREKA!

## THE PLACE I GREW UP

## HOME TRUTHS ABOUT TV

# EUREKA!

## READING

### HE JUST CAN'T STOP INVENTING

Willie Johnson is one of Britain's most successful inventors. He is the man who invented the Micropacer jogging shoe which records time and speed over distance, and the Gogglevox which gives personal television a 'big-screen' effect. Johnson, who lives in a luxurious flat in a converted church, has no scientific background. He relies on design companies and technical experts to translate his ideas into reality.

At an international exhibition of inventions recently, Johnson won nine awards. One of his winners was the Swallet, an electronic wallet which sounds an alarm if a thief cuts the cord around the wearer's neck. Johnson's own personal favourite is the Tantrum. This is a tiny electronic device inside a foam brick. When you throw the brick at your TV set, the device sends a signal to a gadget in the plug socket and turns the electricity off if the set was on or on if it was off.

Johnson had a succession of jobs before he became an inventor twenty years ago. Until the runaway success of the Micropacer in 1984, he struggled to make a living with a string of inventions, from cardboard furniture to a trailer that converted into a boat. 'Sometimes I did well, but for each idea that makes you money you may lose on three or four.' He describes inventing as a tremendous gamble. It costs thousands of pounds to patent an invention, and only one in 1,000 patented ideas will actually become a commercial product. Inventors can either sell an idea outright to a manufacturer or collect a percentage of the sales in royalties. The latter is every inventor's dream and even a simple idea can turn into a pot of gold if it is fun, becomes fashionable, and appeals to young people.

Johnson, whose latest invention is the Wring, a bright plastic ring with a watch that you can change round, believes that his talent lies in taking technological advances and putting them to creative uses that other people have not thought of. Whatever happens, Johnson can't stop inventing.

1 Decide if these statements are true or false according to the text. Give reasons for your answers.

### Glossary

**device:** object that has been invented for a particular purpose

**gadget:** small device that does something useful

**socket:** a place on a wall that you can put an electric plug into

**patent (n):** an official document giving the holder the sole right to make, use or sell an invention and preventing others from imitating it. To patent (v) is to obtain such a document.

**royalties:** sums paid to the owner of a patent or copyright e.g. authors may receive a sum of money for each book sold

*a* Inventors need a technical and scientific background.
*b* Johnson has always found it easy to make a living as an inventor.
*c* Most inventions fail to become commercial products.
*d* Johnson's inventions are based on existing technology.

2 Use your own words to describe how inventors like Johnson make a living.

## VOCABULARY

Suggest alternatives for the words/phrases in *italics*. Try and keep the same meaning.

Example
*luxurious = very comfortable*

*a* a *converted* church
*b* *translate* ideas *into reality*
*c* *awards*
*d* a *succession of* jobs
*e* a *runaway* success
*f* *make a living*
*g* a *string of* inventions
*h* a *tremendous gamble*
*i* a *pot of gold*

## PRONUNCIATION 😐

### Words ending in *-ion*

*-tion*, *-sion*, and *-shion* are all pronounced /ʃən/ in English.

1 Mark the main stress in each of these words.
   creation   invention   fashion
   exhibition   translation

2 Listen and check your answers. Where does the stress normally occur?

3 Listen and repeat.

### Grammar quiz

#### Relative clauses

1 What is the difference between these two relative clauses:

   *a* *He is the man who invented the Micropacer.*
   *b* *Johnson, who lives in a luxurious flat in a converted church, has no scientific background.*

2 When do we use *whose*?
   *Johnson, whose latest invention is the Wring, a bright plastic . . .*

## PRACTICE

1 Rewrite the sentences, using a relative clause to include the information in brackets. The extra information may come in the middle or at the end of the sentence. Do not forget to include the appropriate commas.

a Johnson invented the Soaprise. (It is a ball of soap that floats.)

b 'Eureka!' is used in English when someone suddenly discovers something. (It means 'I have found it' in Greek.)

c The biro or ballpoint-pen was designed for use at high altitudes or underwater. (Its inventor was a Hungarian named Biro.)

d Edison invented the gramophone and the electric light bulb. (He hid himself in a cupboard under the stairs whenever he wanted to solve a problem.)

e The screwdriver was invented before the screw. (It used to be used for removing nails.)

f Charles Babbage is famous for his computers. (He also invented a stethoscope.)

2 Use the prompts to write sentences with *who* or *whose*. Make sure that you include commas where these are appropriate.

a Leonardo Da Vinci be/great inventor /creations included a model of a submarine.

b People/invent things be slightly mad.

c Rubik/best-selling invention be/Cube be also Hungarian.

d Johnson/personal favourite be the Tantrum brick/invent the Micropacer.

e Inventors/not sell ideas/manufacturers often find it difficult/make a living.

## LISTENING 😐

In Britain, there are mail-order companies dedicated to the introduction of the very newest products in the market-place, and to the encouragement of inventors who need a 'launch-pad' for their ideas.

*Streetwise* went to speak to the manager of one of these mail-order companies about some of the products which made it into their catalogue and some which were rejected. Listen to the interview and answer the questions.

1 Complete the grid.

| Name of product | Accepted (Yes/No) | Reason Given (if any) |
|---|---|---|
| a 'jumbo' _____ gauge | | |
| b self-balancing _____ holder | | |
| c car-shaped _____ | | |
| d aerated _____ | | |
| e spectacles for _____ | | |
| f luminous _____ collars | | |
| g jumping _____ | | |
| h motor-powered _____ | | |

2 What criteria do they use for producing the brochure?

3 What criteria do they use for deciding on which products they accept?

## TALKING POINT

Work in small groups.
One of you is an executive in a company that specializes in selling new inventions.

The others are inventors of serious or not so serious products who want to persuade you to sell their products. Unfortunately, there is only room in the catalogue for one product.

The executive should find out as much as possible about the products before coming to a decision.

The inventors should take it in turns to describe their products and persuade the executive to choose their ideas.

# HOME TRUTHS ABOUT TV

## *READING*

### CANDID CAMERAS

Broadcasters like to cultivate the myth of viewers 'glued' to their sets but the pictures here and on the cover show that Britain's most popular programmes often play to total indifference and frequently to nobody at all.

The revealing photographs – the most comprehensive record produced of what goes on in the nation's living rooms – come from 7,000 hours of videotapes made by cameras hidden in 100 British homes and often forgotten by the occupiers. The pictures printed here, and thousands more, offer a frank portrait of a nation for whom television has become a form of electronic wallpaper, usually switched on, but often ignored. They show:

- a man walking out of the room during the news, leaving the prime minister to speak to an empty room.
- a man practising his golf swing during an afternoon chat show.
- top-rated soaps such as Coronation Street playing to nobody.
- a woman cutting her son's hair during a breakfast show.
- a man folding his laundry during a live broadcast of a cricket Test Match.
- a viewer reading a newspaper during a quiz show.

Commercials do even worse, with 20% playing to empty rooms and 10% missed as people used their remote-controls to check out other channels. In fact, half the time, no-one was actually watching the TV set.

Using video cameras hidden inside the televisions, Dr Peter Collett was able to see what was going on. Collett said:

'We have suffered from illusions about the nature of the television viewer for a long time, born of the convenience of the television contractors and advertising agencies. What they've managed to do is to conjure up an image of an essentially passive viewer who is therefore amenable to the messages of the advertisers and programme makers. The tapes show this is simply not the case. Viewers are very active. If they don't like something they'll switch off, or else they'll engage in some other activity or not pay attention.'

### Glossary

**conjure up an image of:** create a picture in your mind of

**amenable to (the messages):** willing to receive

The research is hotly contested by broadcasting executives who claim the research does not reflect what the majority actually do. What do you think?

*a* Use a maximum of fifty words to summarize the main ideas in the text.

*b* Dr Collett's research has been used to persuade advertisers to choose newspapers rather than television. Why?

## *VOCABULARY*

Find expressions in the text with similar meanings to the following.

*a* try hard to develop an untrue idea
*b* watching television with their full attention
*c* a complete lack of interest
*d* the pictures providing new facts
*e* an honest representation of
*f* have been badly affected by false beliefs and ideas
*g* not the actual state of affairs
*h* strongly objected to

---

### *Improve your wordpower*

*1* Rewrite these informal expressions in plain English.

*a* What's on telly?
*b* He was on the box last night.

*2* What would you expect to see in a typical example of one of these types of television programme?

*a* soap
*b* documentary
*c* chat show
*d* game show
*e* live broadcast
*f* situation comedy
*g* magazine programme
*h* variety show
*i* thriller
*j* costume drama

---

## *TALKING POINT*

Carry out a class survey to answer these questions:

*a* Does Dr Collett's research reflect what people do while they watch television in your country or not?

*b* Does what people do while they are watching television depend on the type of programme they are watching or not?

## Improve your grammar

### Participle Clauses

Participle clauses are mainly used in written English. The clause can be introduced by the *-ing* form of the verb ...

*Opening the window, he leant outside.*

... or the participle with *-ed*.

*Bored by the programme, he fell asleep.*

Some of the most common uses are as follows:

*1* To describe how or why something happened:

*Using video cameras hidden inside the television, Collett was able to ...*

*Accused of dishonesty by the media, the minister decided to resign.*

*2* To replace defining relative clauses:

*The pictures show a man who is folding his laundry ...*

*The pictures show a man folding his laundry ...*

*A scientist who is known as 'Superman' ...*

*A scientist known as 'Superman' ...*

*3* With certain link words, like *when, whenever, before, after, while, since.*

*Since starting his research ...*

*After saying goodbye, he left.*

## PRACTICE

*1* Rewrite these sentences with an *-ing* form participle clause. Make any necessary changes.

Example

*Since Dr Collett completed his research, he has become quite famous.*

*Since completing his research, Dr Collett has become quite famous.*

*a* The programme which is being broadcast is the nine o'clock news.

*b* Alexandra pointed at the stranger and said he reminded her of her maths teacher.

*c* While Collett's assistant was looking through the research photographs, he saw a picture of his uncle.

*d* While he was looking through the videotapes, Collett noticed that many people did not concentrate on the programmes.

*e* He forgot about the camera, so he came into the room without his clothes on.

*f* The group worked steadily all morning and finished at noon.

## GETTING STREETWISE!
### Criticizing

*1* What do you think of television? *Streetwise* discovered that many of its readers are critical about television. Listen to what they said and:

*a* note the main areas of complaint.

*b* tick the expressions used.

*I've had enough of ...*
*I'm fed up with ...*
*It's all their fault that ...*
*It gets on my nerves.*
*It's about time ..., isn't it?*
*They could at least have ...*
*You shouldn't ...*
*Why couldn't they ...?*

Remember that these are informal expressions which are quite strong. It would be best to avoid using them to criticize strangers, complain in shops, etc. They can be used with people you know well or with strangers when you are all complaining about the same thing, e.g. when a bus which is often late is late again.

*2* Work in a small group. Start by checking your answers. Now use the expressions in your list to write down what people would say if they were asked to criticize television in your country.

## WRITING

What do you think of foreign films and television programmes? Are they better than local programmes or not? Are they a good or a bad influence? Why/Why not?

Write an opinion piece in which you give your views on foreign films and programmes.

# THE PLACE I GREW UP

## WARM-UP

Which of these brief descriptions is closer to the place where you were born? Why? Write down what you remember most about the place where you spent the first few years of your life.

'When I was a child I lived in a place where, for most of the year, you could walk for eight or nine hours without seeing a human being'.

'We lived in a block of flats which had forty apartments. Although our nearest neighbours were six inches away we never spoke to them'.

## READING ☺

A man is talking about his childhood. Read this description and answer the questions.

By the time I was seven we were living in the same farmhouse that my parents are living in now. I think I was happy there. It was a fairly big farmhouse with thick walls which were crumbly. In fact some of the walls were so crumbly that at one point, my bedroom had a hole that went all the way through to the outside.

*Glossary*

**crumbly:** easily broken into lots of little pieces

**sink:** large basin in kitchen used for washing plates, cups, etc.

The kitchen had this sink that was carved out of stone and there was a stove in the corner where there was always something cooking. Next to the kitchen there was a stairway and then at the front of the house there were a couple of fairly big sitting rooms, one that we used all the time and one for special occasions. At the top of the stairs there were two little bedrooms and a bathroom. I don't remember having much of an opinion about living on the farm. The farm was just something that was there. It wasn't altogether great being the only kid around. I think my best friend – I don't know if this was at seven or a little bit older – was a 15-year-old who came to work for my father. He was the nearest person to my age there, so I used to follow him around and I was terribly upset when he left and got another job.

*a*  Where did the writer grow up?
*b*  What is your impression of the place where he lived?
*c*  Do you think he had a lonely childhood? In what way? Give reasons for your answer.
*d*  Describe the similarities and differences between the writer's description of his childhood home and what you remember about your own.

## TALKING POINT

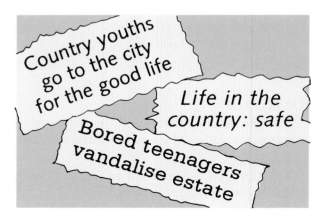

Prepare to take part in a debate on the motion:
*The countryside is an ideal place to grow up.*

*a*  Decide whether you want to speak for or against the motion.
*b*  Work with other students on the same side and list your main arguments.
*c*  Now list the arguments you think your opponents will use. Think of objections to them.
*d*  Decide on the order in which you will speak. Make sure each of you presents part of your argument.

## Improve your wordpower

1 Match the names to the pictures.
   flat (or apartment)   mansion
   cottage   hut   bungalow

2 Which of these adjectives would you
   apply to these houses/homes?
   derelict   luxurious   old-fashioned
   high-rise   single-storey

3 In this context, what is the opposite of:
   luxurious   old-fashioned   derelict

## PRACTICE

1 Use *where, who, which* to join these
  sentences.
  Example
  I lived in a villa. It was old. It was near the
  beach.
  *I lived in an old villa which was near the
  beach.*

  a The street was crowded. It was dirty. It was
    full of traffic.
  b I lived in a house. It was huge. It was very
    cold in winter.
  c My neighbours lived four kilometres away.
    They were very nice.
  d The place I grew up in was quiet. It was
    boring. It was a village.
  e The hospital was very old. It was very
    beautiful. It was next door to our house.

2 Join each pair of sentences by using a
  participle clause.
  Example
  I lived in an old house. It was built of stone.
  *I lived in an old house, built of stone.*

  a They lived in a villa. The villa was painted
    white to reflect the sun.
  b The flats were very convenient. They were
    built near a bus stop.
  c He lives in a small flat. He has lived there
    since he moved to New York.
  d He remembered the house he was born in.
    He smiled happily.

3 Fill in each gap with a word from this box.

> built   room   sun   stone   started
> pale   solid   which   from   strong
> wooden   attached

The house was a farmhouse _____ (a) from
local stone. Two hundred years of wind and
_____ (b) had turned the stone to a colour
somewhere between pale honey and _____ (c)
grey. It had _____ (d) life in the eighteenth
century as one _____ (e), and it had spread
until it had become an irregular three-storey
house. Everything about it was _____ (f).
The spiral staircase, _____ (g) rose from the
wine cellar to the top floor, was cut _____ (h)
massive slabs of stone. The walls, some of
them a metre thick, were built to keep out
the _____ (i) cold northern winds which,
they say, can blow the ears off a donkey.
_____ (j) to the back of the house was a
courtyard, and beyond that a white _____ (k)
swimming pool. In the afternoon sun, with
the _____ (l) shutters half-closed like sleepy
eyelids, it was irresistible.

## Improve your writing

### Describing places

a Select a viewpoint for your description.
  Is the description personal?
  *We were living in … The house was …*
  Or neutral?
  *Skye is a small island …*
  Are you trying to describe the whole
  picture or part of it? Are you concerned
  with something general or with detail?

b Create the atmosphere by describing
  some of the things in detail.
  *There was a stove in the corner where
  there was always something cooking.
  … thick walls which were crumbly …*

c If possible help the reader create a
  picture of the place by using images.
  *shutters half-closed like sleepy eyelids*

d If the description is personal you should
  include your feelings about the place.
  *It reminds me of …
  I makes me feel …
  I remember …*

## WRITING
Write a personal description of a place you
love.

# LANGUAGE AND GENDER

## READING

### My son, my son

1 Arrange these sentences in the correct order to tell a story.

'My son,' cried the surgeon, horrified, 'that's my son!'
There was a road accident.
The surgeon at the hospital recognized the boy.
The father was killed outright.
The boy was taken to hospital.
A lorry ran over a man and his son.

2 Who is the surgeon? What problems, if any, did you have in doing the task?

### Man

3 Read this sentence.

*Man needs food and water to survive.*

Now close your eyes. Did you visualize both sexes or only men? In research, most people visualized only men. This suggests that the use of *man* (to mean 'all humans') can promote a one-sided view of the world. For example, what does this sentence suggest?

*Businessmen should be good at managing money.*

When occupations are being discussed in general terms many users try to replace job titles which include *man* with natural alternatives. Here are some examples.

businessman → executive
fireman → fire fighter
foreman → supervisor
policeman → police officer
statesman → leader, politician

4 Suggest alternatives for these expressions.
headmaster
mankind
manpower
man-made
prehistoric man

## TALKING POINT

### Hidden Meanings

Comment on the images of men and women implied in these examples of communication.

*a* The mummies on the bus go chatter, chatter, chatter.
The daddies on the bus go read, read, read.

From a nursery rhyme *The wheels on the bus*.

*b*

Hello, Mr Jones. You're looking gorgeous as usual. Go and get me a coffee, would you, sweetie?

*c* Jenny Craig, attractive Los Angeles lawyer, began her defence of . . .
From a newspaper

*d*

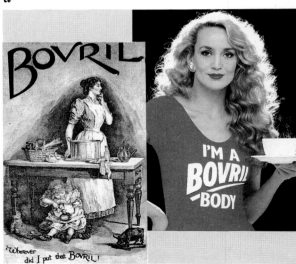

BOVRIL

Whatever did I put that BOVRIL!

I'M A BOVRIL BODY

### Research

*Aim:*

1) to analyse a magazine to see how men and women are treated in it. You could look at things like:
*the hidden meanings of illustrations*
*the number of men and women shown*
*the kinds of jobs men and women do*

# GRAMMAR REVIEW ISSUES 11 AND 12

## REPORTED SPEECH

### 1 Tense changes

When the reporting verb is in the past (*said, told*, etc.) there are usually tense changes in reported speech.

| Direct speech | Reported speech |
|---|---|
| Simple present | Simple past |
| Present progressive | Past progressive |
| Present perfect simple | Past perfect simple |
| Present perfect progressive | Past perfect progressive |
| Simple past | Past perfect |
| Will | Would |

**Examples**

| | |
|---|---|
| *'I'm working.'* | *She said she was working.* |
| *'He has seen it already.'* | *She said he had seen it already.* |
| *'Jack will do it.'* | *She said Jack would do it.* |

**Exceptions**

*a* If the verb in direct speech is in the past, we often leave it in the past in reported speech, unless we want to emphasize the fact that one event happened before another.

> *'I left at six.'*  *He said he left at six.*

*b* We do not usually change a simple present tense if the statement is always true.

> *'The sun rises in the east.'*  *He said that the sun rises in the east.*

### 2 No tense changes

There are no tense changes when we report direct speech with a verb in the present (*say, tell*, etc.). We may choose this when we report a conversation that is still going on, e.g. when someone is talking on the phone, when reading a letter to report what it says, when reading instructions and reporting them, and when reporting something a person says all the time.

*This postcard is from Steve and Gaby. They say they're having a great time.*

*'What do the instructions say?' 'They say cut along the dotted line.'*

### 3 Reported questions

The most common verbs for reporting questions are *ask*, *want to know* and *inquire*.

We report *yes/no* questions with *if* or *whether*.

| | |
|---|---|
| *Do you like tea?* | *He asked me if I liked tea.* |

When reporting *wh-* questions we use question words.

| | |
|---|---|
| *Why do you like tea?* | *He asked me why I liked tea.* |

### 4 Reporting the gist

Here are some verbs that allow us to report the gist:

| | | | |
|---|---|---|---|
| accept | grumble | mutter | respond |
| beg | invite | offer | threaten |
| complain | moan | promise | warn |
| deny | mumble | refuse | |

It is possible to report a conversation by giving the gist of what was said rather than the exact words.

*He invited us to dinner and we accepted.*

## GERUND AND INFINITIVE

### 1
Some verbs are followed by the *-ing* form. Here are the most common:

| | | |
|---|---|---|
| admit | can't stand | feel like |
| appreciate | deny | finish |
| avoid | dislike | hate |
| be used to | dread | keep (= continue) |
| can't help | enjoy | miss |

*I can't stand seeing people suffer.*
*He hates getting up early.*

### 2
Some verbs are followed by the infinitive (base form) with *to*. Here are some of the most common.

| | | | |
|---|---|---|---|
| afford | fail | learn | prepare |
| appear | forget | manage | promise |
| arrange | happen | mean | refuse |
| choose | hope | offer | seem |
| decide | intend | plan | threaten |

*I offered to help them.*
*They're preparing to leave.*

### 3
A few verbs take either *-ing* or *to* with a change of meaning.

**stop**

*a* *I stopped going to the gym a few weeks ago.* (= I went to the gym until a few weeks ago, then I stopped.)

*b* *I stopped to go the gym on the way home.* (= I was on my way home and I stopped in order to visit the gym).

**remember**

*a* *I remembered going to the party.* (= I remember doing this in the past.)

*I remembered to go to the party.* (= I remembered the invitation and I went to the party.)

**try**

a  *I tried taking an aspirin.*
   (= I did an experiment.)
b  *I tried to take an aspirin.* (= I made an
   effort.)

**go on**

a  *After he left school, he went on to study
   Maths at university.* (= one action followed
   another)
b  *We went on studying after the end of the
   lesson.* (= We continued studying.)

## *RELATIVE CLAUSES*
### Defining and non-defining

1  In defining relative clauses we learn which woman,
   man, car, etc., the speaker is talking about.
   *I spoke to the man who lives next door.*

2  'Non-defining' relative clauses do not tell us which
   person, thing, etc., the speaker means; these clauses
   give us extra, but not absolutely necessary
   information.

   *I like my Uncle Jim, who owns four dogs.*
   *Johnson, who lives next door, is an inventor.*

   These are most common in writing.
   When we write these we put commas (,) around the
   relative clause, except when it comes at the end of the
   sentence.

## *PARTICIPLE CLAUSES*
Participle clauses are mainly used in written English.
The clause can be introduced by the *-ing* form of the
verb, or the past participle.

*Opening the window, he leant out and . . .*
*Bored by the film, she fell asleep in the cinema.*

Some of the most common uses of participle clauses are
as follows:

1  To describe how or why something happened.
   *Using video cameras hidden inside the TV, Collett
   was able to . . .*
   *Accused of dishonesty by the media, the minister
   resigned.*

2  To replace defining relative clauses.
   *The pictures show a man who is folding his laundry.*
   *The pictures show a man folding his laundry.*
   *A scientist who is known as 'Superman' . . .*
   *A scientist known as 'Superman' . . .*

3  With certain link words, like *when, whenever,
   before, after, while, since.*
   *Since starting his research, Collett has found . . .*
   *After saying goodbye, he left.*

# GRAMMAR PRACTICE

*A*

1  Rewrite each of these sentences so that you keep the
   same meaning. Start with the words given.

a  'Where is the nearest restaurant?' asked the tourist.
   The tourist _____ .
b  'Stop and don't go any further,' said the policeman.
   The policeman ordered them _____ .
c  Charles said, 'I haven't seen Ann for years.'
   Charles told me _____ .
d  Helen told me that she liked him.
   Helen said '_____ .'
e  'Are you alone?' Chris asked.
   Chris wanted _____ .
f  'Tom saw me on his way to work,' he said.
   He told me _____ .
g  She said she had worked in Australia two years ago.
   Margaret said '_____ .'

2  Join the two sentences using *who, which* or *whose.*
   Make any changes that are necessary.

   Example
   That's Mary. Her sister is my teacher.
   *That's Mary whose sister is my teacher.*

a  That is Alan. I saw him at the match.
b  The Baiji is a dolphin. It lives in the Yangtze.
c  She is the girl. Her walkman was stolen.
d  Do you know that boy? Alan is talking to him.
e  I rented a bike. It was green.
f  Those are the people. Their dog is the same as ours.
g  I spoke Alice. She is in your class.

3  Put the verbs in brackets into either *-ing* or *to* + base
   form.

a  Did you remember _____ (stop) and buy me a
   hamburger?
b  I forgot _____ (remind) him.
c  Why don't you try _____ (wear) green socks
   with that suit?
d  They stopped _____ (go) to violin lessons when
   they left school.
e  I'm sorry I forgot _____ (bring) your book.
f  I'll remember _____ (send) you a postcard from
   Germany.
g  First, he had a job in a shop. Then he went on
   _____ (work) in a garage.
h  I asked him to stop, but he went on _____ (sing).

## B

1 Complete the sentences with an -ing form or past participle of the verbs below.

make   walk   do   know   leave   sell   lie   say

a He is ____ as a hard worker.
b The painting shows a woman ____ her washing.
c I gave money to the people ____ homeless by the war.
d The people ____ to the match were singing.
e Look at that dog ____ in the middle of the road.
f He only buys clothes ____ at half price.
g Since ____ university, he has got himself a good job.
h He left after ____ hello to a few people.

2 Join each pair of sentences using a present participle.
   Example
   Who is that man? He is speaking to my sister.
   *Who is that man speaking to my sister?*

a There is a crowd outside the concert hall. They are waiting to see Jason.
b My little brother hurt himself. He was trying to climb a high wall.
c John broke his leg. He was running down the stairs.
d The dog was crossing the road. It was hit by a car.
e I arrived home at midnight. I wasn't feeling very well.

3 Finish each of the following sentences in such a way that it means the same as the sentence before it.

a Did I see him? I don't remember.
   I don't remember _____ .
b 'Let's go waterskiing next week,' said John.
   John suggested _____ .
c My teacher gets angry when students sleep in class.
   My teacher can't stand _____ .
d The little boy said that he had hadn't taken the cake.
   The little boy denied _____ .
e I have enough money to buy a new stereo.
   I can afford _____ .
f He did not succeed in passing the exam.
   He failed _____ .

4 Use verbs in the list to report what was said in each situation.

warn   invite   deny   accept   threaten   offer   grumble

## C

1 Tell a pen friend about TV in your country. Your letter should answer these questions:

a What is the most popular programme?
b Who is the most popular television personality?
c What is your favourite programme?
d What is the most boring programme?
e Which is the most popular soap opera?
f Which programmes do young people like ?
   Example
   *The most popular programme in the UK is Coronation Street, which is a soap opera.*

2

This is the last line of a conversation between the people in the picture. Continue this report of the conversation that led up to it.

Last night, I was listening to music in my room. Dad came up to my room and . . .

# Wise up!

# WRITING

## THE WRITING PROCESS

There are several stages in almost any piece of writing:

Stage 1: Generating ideas
Stage 2: Planning
Stage 3: Drafting and re-drafting
Stage 4: Presenting your work

Here is a possible approach.

- Start by generating as many ideas as possible. You may wish to use a diagram. Here is an example for the topic: *Children shouldn't be allowed to work. Discuss.*

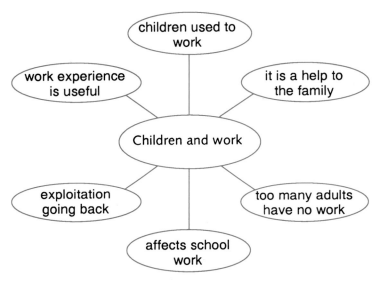

- You need to make a plan. This will depend on the kind of writing you need to produce. In this example, the topic calls for a discussion, so you would probably group the ideas you have generated into arguments FOR and AGAINST the topic. You will plan better if you become familiar with the general structure of the main types of writing. The *Improve your writing* boxes in *Streetwise* should help you with this.
- Start writing.
- Read back over what you have written to make sure that it is correct, that words are spelled correctly, and that you've said all that you want to say. If you have time, write out a clean version of your first draft. Remember to write clearly and check your spelling and grammar. Use correction fluid if this is available.

1 You have been asked to write a talk welcoming a group of visitors to your town. Work in pairs and make a plan of the main points you will include in your talk. Share your ideas with the class.

2 Discuss the advantages and disadvantages of the suggested method of planning and decide on the approach that suits you.

## BECOMING A BETTER WRITER

Your ability to write will improve with practice. At the same time you can help yourself by:

- reading as much English as possible
- studying the way model essays are organized
- learning to check your own work quickly and efficiently
- building up a stock of useful phrases
- trying to write within a strict time limit

1 Choose one of these types of writing and brainstorm a stock of useful phrases for:

a  formal letters          c  a discussion essay
b  informal letters        d  a summary

## WHAT THE EXAMINER WANTS

The questions and tasks in a writing exam are designed so that candidates can produce a piece of writing at the level required by the exam. Examiners may look at areas such as:

- the accuracy of grammar, spelling and punctuation
- the range of vocabulary and grammar
- the general organization of the writing
- the relevance and appropriacy of the answer

... but the key is to write clearly and effectively.

1 Some students were asked to write a letter complaining about a stereo that stopped working when it was taken home from the shop. What is wrong with these extracts?

Dear Sir
I am really angry that it does not work. I have never had so many problems with a new machine. . .

Dear Sir
I bought a new stereo. When we plugged it in, it blew up and frightened me and the cat.

Dear Sir
I beg to inform you that the stereo I bought has ceased to operate ever since I brought it to my domicile.

## TYPES OF WRITING

As part of a writing exam you might be required to produce:

personal notes and messages, formal and informal letters, reports, reviews, stories and anecdotes, opinion pieces, instructions, a summary, etc.

It is therefore very important that you recognize the type of writing required by a question, and read any parts of the exam paper where you have a choice at least twice before you decide what to do.

1   Look at these examples of exam questions and decide what type of writing is required by each one.

a   You have heard of a scholarship to go to Britain to improve your English. Write a letter applying for the scholarship.

b   Describe how you learned to swim.

c   Children shouldn't be allowed to work. Discuss.

d   You were going to a concert with a friend. Unfortunately you have had to change your plans. Write and explain why.

e   Write an account of a concert or film that you have been to.

# IRREGULAR VERBS

| Base form | Simple past | Past participle | Base form | Simple past | Past Participle |
|-----------|-------------|-----------------|-----------|-------------|-----------------|
| be | was/were | been | make | made | made |
| beat | beat | beaten | mean | meant | meant |
| become | became | become | meet | met | met |
| begin | began | begun | pay | paid | paid |
| bend | bent | bent | put | put | put |
| bite | bit | bitten | read | read | read |
| blow | blew | blown | ride | rode | ridden |
| break | broke | broken | ring | rang | rung |
| bring | brought | brought | rise | rose | risen |
| build | built | built | run | ran | run |
| burn | burnt | burnt | say | said | said |
| buy | bought | bought | see | saw | seen |
| catch | caught | caught | sell | sold | sold |
| choose | chose | chosen | send | sent | sent |
| come | came | come | set | set | set |
| cost | cost | cost | shake | shook | shaken |
| cut | cut | cut | shine | shone | shone |
| dig | dug | dug | shoot | shot | shot |
| do | did | done | show | showed | shown |
| draw | drew | drawn | shrink | shrank | shrunk |
| dream | dreamt | dreamt | shut | shut | shut |
| drink | drank | drunk | sing | sang | sung |
| drive | drove | driven | sink | sank | sunk |
| eat | ate | eaten | sit | sat | sat |
| fall | fell | fallen | sleep | slept | slept |
| feed | fed | fed | slide | slid | slid |
| feel | felt | felt | smell | smelt | smelt |
| find | found | found | speak | spoke | spoken |
| fly | flew | flown | spell | spelt | spelt |
| forget | forgot | forgotten | spill | spilt | spilt |
| freeze | froze | frozen | spend | spent | spent |
| get | got | got | stand | stood | stood |
| give | gave | given | steal | stole | stolen |
| go | went | gone (been) | sting | stung | stung |
| have | had | had | strike | struck | struck |
| hear | heard | heard | swear | swore | sworn |
| hide | hid | hidden | swim | swam | swum |
| hit | hit | hit | take | took | taken |
| hold | held | held | teach | taught | taught |
| hurt | hurt | hurt | tear | tore | torn |
| keep | kept | kept | tell | told | told |
| know | knew | known | think | thought | thought |
| lay | laid | laid | throw | threw | thrown |
| learn | learnt | learnt | understand | understood | understood |
| leave | left | left | wake | woke | woken |
| lend | lent | lent | wear | wore | worn |
| let | let | let | weep | wept | wept |
| lie | lay | lain | win | won | won |
| lose | lost | lost | write | wrote | written |